Growing Up
In
Glitter Gulch

By: Darrin S. Bush

Table of Contents

Dedication

This book is for my wife, Debbie, and my wonderful family. You have made my life complete.

Acknowledgments

I want to thank Marc and Gwen for their support and encouragement. There are special stories in this book dedicated to the fabulous Mamie Van Doren. You are truly my friend for life.

About the Author

Darrin Bush was born and raised in Las Vegas. He attended Saint Joseph elementary school, Bishop Gorman High School and the University of Nevada at Reno. In 1970 he began his working life in the hospitality industry at the Sahara and Frontier hotels, where he was Room Service Manager, Food and Beverage Manager and Executive Slot Host. In 1988, he turned his passion for photography into a career, and became a photographer for the Las Vegas News Bureau.

Darrin spent 26 years behind the lens of his camera capturing headline entertainers, scenic landscapes, world-class sporting events and the ever-evolving Las Vegas skyline. He completed more than 7,000 photo assignments, and contributed over 400,000 images to the archives of Las Vegas. The Associated Press, Reuters, Getty Images and Agence French Press have distributed Darrin's work worldwide.

He has published in the New York Times, USA Today, Los Angeles Times and the Wall Street Journal. His photography has received honors for marketing Las Vegas from the Professional Photographers of America, the MarCom Creative Awards and Galaxy Awards. Darrin also published four books of poetry and two coffee table photo books. He received the Key to The City from Mayor Oscar

B. Goodman in 2010, and was featured on the PBS television series "ArtScene" in 2014.

Darrin's photos were presented in the June, 2015 edition of Desert Companion's on-line magazine, the article entitled "Fire in the sky: images of an ever-changing Strip." In 2016, Darrin was a participant in the University of Nevada Las Vegas Oral History Department's project entitled "Building Las Vegas." Mr. Bush is considered a Las Vegas historian.

Foreword

Darrin Bush is a skilled photographer, accomplished poet, and talented memoirist. He's an amazing writer and the nicest person I know. It wouldn't surprise me to learn that Darrin can sink 8 out of 10 baskets from the 3-point line, turn a fast double play from shortstop, or shoot in the low 80s on the golf course. Darrin is truly a Renaissance Man.

Did I mention he's a terrific writer? As you read Growing Up In Glitter Gulch, he'll slyly slip you into the milieu of the good old Las Vegas days Darrin saw while growing up. The pages of GUiGG are filled with fascinating anecdotes of Vegas' most famous and infamous—names you'll know and names you'll wish you did. If Darrin didn't know everybody, he damn well knew someone who did.

In 2001, when Darrin was with the Las Vegas News Bureau, he took a working vacation to Newport Beach, toting stacks of vintage press photos of people no one could identify. Darrin enlisted Las Vegas veteran and comedian Joey Bishop, who lived just a few blocks from me. Darrin remarked that he once read that Mamie Van Doren lived in Newport Beach, too, and wondered if Joey knew how to get in touch with her. Joey said, "Hell yes! She lives just down the street."

And so it was that Kismet brought Darrin and me together to become fast friends while spending a hilarious afternoon with Joey, cracking one-liners about the unknowns and barely knowns in Darrin's clippings. I would go on to meet and love Darrin's beautiful wife, Debbie, and his lovely daughter Heather. It would have been enough just to have known Darrin and the Bushes. But with this delightful book as an added attraction, it's the icing on the cake. Read this, and you'll become Darrin's friend too. You'll be glad you did.

Mamie Van Doren

Newport Beach, California

January 5, 2023

Chapter 1: The Adventure Begins

I believe that all of us have life-long journeys filled with both joy and tragedy. I have certainly had my share of both. Each story in this book is a small piece of the puzzle that shaped my life. My birth certificate says that I was born at Clark County General Hospital on January 8, 1948. I don't remember that particular event, so I'll begin my story in a different way.

My mother's name was Marianne Kanis. Her parents were immigrants from Czechoslovakia. They did not speak English, nor did they have any money. All they had was the dream of a decent life. They settled in western Pennsylvania next to a dairy farm. They had a large family and lived a very meager lifestyle. Some of the boys worked in steel mills, while others enlisted in the army. The girls raised crops and worked around the house. Mom would tell me stories of the dairy farm. She was fascinated with its sounds and smells when she was young. As she grew older, her love of rural life diminished. She was about seventeen when she rode a train to California with her friend, Patty.

Mom told me it was a troop train because it was during World War Two, and the train was filled with army troops. What money she had was hidden in her hair, and Patty protected her from the guys. When they arrived in Hollywood, mom got a day job as a waitress in a cafeteria where the movie-stars ate. She actually began hanging out with The Three Stooges. She went bowling with them on Friday nights. Maybe that's why I inherited my appreciation for sophisticated humor. By night, she worked as a camera girl in a place where celebrities frequently dined. It was either the Brown Derby or the Trocadero. She said her favorite movie star was Robert Taylor. She photographed him a few times, and he always gave her a nice tip. I wish she had told me more about her life. Unfortunately, she kept most of it to herself.

She had several dates in those days but only mentioned Moe, Larry, and Curly. After a few years in Hollywood, she got married and moved to Las Vegas. Her husband pursued a career in entertainment management, among other things. He also became one of Sheriff Ralph Lamb's best friends. I was born in 1948, after which my father soon left us. After that, Mom did the best she could. She was suddenly a single parent.

My mother used to walk me down Fremont Street in a stroller. She said that people would throw silver dollars into the stroller for no reason. It must have made them feel good. In those days, everybody had silver dollars instead of paper money. Maybe that's why Downtown Las Vegas became known as "Glitter Gulch." It was an irresistible place, filled with neon signs and smoky casinos. The hotels had names like El Cortez, Pioneer Club, Las Vegas Club, Horseshoe,

Golden Nugget, and Lucky Strike Club. Their owners became gambling icons. Jackie Gaughan, Benny Binion, and Sam Boyd were the Founding Fathers of Downtown. There were no shopping malls or freeways, just the glittering lights of Fremont Street. Las Vegas, Nevada, was truly the Wild West.

When I was three years old, mom took me to Pennsylvania with her friend named Bea. They were both from there, so they made the long drive to their homeland to visit relatives. Bea had a new Chevrolet, and that's the car they used. They would take turns driving, and I rode in the back. After six days of sightseeing, we arrived at our destination. Bea dropped us off at my grandparent's house in Leechburg. Most of the people in that area were either coal miners or steel workers. Before she passed away, mom told me that there was a gun under the passenger seat of Bea's car. They felt safe on their travels. As a teenager, I continued

5

my visits to Pennsylvania. Mom's brother John drove his family to our house in the summer of 1965. After their visit, I drove back with them. This time, I was in a new Pontiac. In those days, everyone drove American cars. Mom had a lot of brothers and sisters, but John was her favorite. He was the oldest and had the most responsibility. He was also a veteran of World War Two. Like many of his fellow Marines, he picked up Malaria while fighting at Guadalcanal. It bothered him for the rest of his life.

The hotels on the Las Vegas Strip, known as Highway 91, were larger and more glamorous than the ones Downtown. In 1941 the El Rancho Vegas was the first hotel to open on Las Vegas Boulevard South. It was built on a large section of land and had a beautiful swimming pool. A year later, a western-style hotel called the Last Frontier was opened just down the street. In 1946, Ben Siegel opened the fabulous Flamingo. The Thunderbird debuted in 1948, followed by the Desert Inn in 1950. There were two hotel openings in 1952, the Sahara and the Sands. Las Vegas became a boomtown when the Riviera and the Dunes welcomed customers in 1955. Two years later, the Strip was enriched with the dazzling Tropicana Hotel. Because of legalized gambling, a mild climate, and plenty of rooms, Las Vegas was suddenly a well-known and desirable destination.

Most of the Strip hotels invested in luxurious boats, which were kept at the marina on Lake Mead. The boats were probably Chris-Craft cabin cruisers. They stood out from the smaller motorboats because of their size and beauty. Each boat had a hotel's logo painted on the front in large letters. I remember seeing the boats leaving the marina and wishing I was on them. The El Rancho, Thunderbird, Dunes, and Desert Inn boats were a sight to behold. After a few years, the hotels realized that their customers belonged in the casinos rather than on Lake Mead. Little by little, the boats disappeared.

Mom's first job in Las Vegas was at Ben Siegel's Flamingo Hotel. She was a cocktail girl at the swimming pool. One day she asked Mr. Siegel if she could transfer into the casino, where there was more money to be made. He told her that she would have to stay at the pool because she was too short. She ultimately quit and got a job at the Last Frontier. She was happy with her work and rented a small house in the Huntridge section of town. She worked nights, so she put me in a group home on Clark Way Drive. It was right behind Binion's Ranch, just off Bonanza Road. The lady who owned the house was named Zuggy, short for Mrs. Zugg. She took in children, and I lived with her for a few years. At that time, it seemed like country living. There were a lot of trees in the area, and the Binion family owned horses. I used to walk around the neighborhood with the other kids and watch the activity at the ranch. It was actually a pretty good life. Mom would visit or take me to her house on her days off. In 1955 mom married Bob Bush, and they bought a new house in Twin Lakes. My brother Marc was born in 1956, and the family started.

Most of my mom's friends were gals she met while working on the Strip. Toddy and Jane Dillard, Peggy De Gregorio, and Fern Benson were the ones she was closest to. They were cocktail girls from such places as the Castaways, the Frontier, the Silver Slipper, and the Flamingo. When they had holiday parties, mom always took me. At first, I was the little man about town. Later, they taught me how to mix cocktails. By the time I was a teenager, I was a pretty good bartender. I knew everybody's favorite drink and how to make it. Since I didn't drink, I relied on their word that the cocktails were OK. I have been surrounded by cocktail girls all my life. It's a gift and a curse.

Mom told me about a strange animal incident that happened at the Last Frontier hotel. She was working the night shift when a bobcat wandered into the casino. Since there was nothing but vacant land behind the hotel, it was easy for the large cat to meander in. The story goes that people started to panic, so a security guard pulled out his gun and shot the bobcat beside a craps table. True or not, that's a unique Las Vegas tale.

In my younger years, Twin Lakes was my domain. I knew every nook and cranny of the neighborhood, and my parents knew most of the people on our street. As I grew older, I expanded my horizons beyond the nearby horse stables, swimming pool, and shopping center. I ventured to faraway places, like Downtown and the Strip. I had dinner at fancy restaurants such as the Alpine Village, the House of Lords, and Bob Taylor's Ranch. Twin Lakes was one of the first self-contained resorts in town. It had horse stables, fishing ponds, streams, motel rooms, fruit trees, and a very large swimming pool. The horses were true stable horses. You had to force them to leave the stables. Otherwise, they would run back to their stalls. I don't know if they were lazy or just smarter than me. Either way, the stables were where they wanted to be. The pool was so big that it had its own island. For young boys, swimming to the island was a transition into manhood, and we were very proud of the achievement. It was not only the largest pool in the state; it was also the coldest. We used to catch crawdads in the streams and ride paddle boats on the lakes. The boats were kind of awkward, but they were fun anyway. Twin Lakes was a wonderful place. People could buy a season pass to the swimming pool during the summer or just arrive at their leisure. For me, it was more than a neighborhood. It was a way of life.

Peggy and Syl DeGregorio lived around the block from us in Twin Lakes. Peggy was a cocktail girl at the Flamingo, and Syl worked at the Golden Gate. They had two boys, Lou and Chick, and a female boxer. Eventually, the dog had puppies, and we picked one out of the litter. We brought the beautiful puppy home and named her Sheba. She quickly became my parent's worst nightmare. Among other things, she tore the clothes off of mom's clothesline and ruined the Slip-N-Slide. Soon after that, she ran through the screen door with her sister, Hortence. Ultimately, they got rid of the boxer. It was many years until they had another dog.

Dogs were always prevalent in Las Vegas. In fact, the Sands Hotel sponsored a popular event during the 1960s called The Poodle Parade. On Easter Sunday, Las Vegas residents that owned poodles would dress their dogs in costumes and gather around the hotel's swimming pool. One by one, the dogs and their owners would show off their designs. Most of the time, the owners dressed in the same ensemble as the dogs. It was a unique fashion show. They were judged and awarded prizes. One year, our neighbors, Lou and Chick, dressed like sailors and proudly walked their poodle in the parade. I don't remember whether they won a prize. It was a great community event.

There was one neighbor on our street that my mom often mentioned. His name was Jacob "Shorty" Manch. He was a Lieutenant Colonel in the United States Air Force and a member of Jimmy Doolittle's Raiders. On April 18, 1942, Jimmy Doolittle led 16 B-25 bombers from the U.S. Navy aircraft carrier Hornet in a spectacular surprise attack on Japan. Shorty Manch was part of that raid. I never met Mr. Manch, but my parents did. Colonel Manch was killed in a flying accident near Nellis Air force Base in 1958. Today, the Jacob E. Manch Elementary School in Las Vegas is named in his honor.

During that time, Las Vegas had its share of television celebrities. Jack Kogan, Gus Giuffre, and G.L. Vitto hosted afternoon or late-night movies. There were also popular radio personalities, such as Red McIlvaine and Coffee Jim Dandy, who worked for AM stations. In those days, there weren't many F.M. stations. As I look back, I realize that nobody actually knew Coffee Jim's real name.

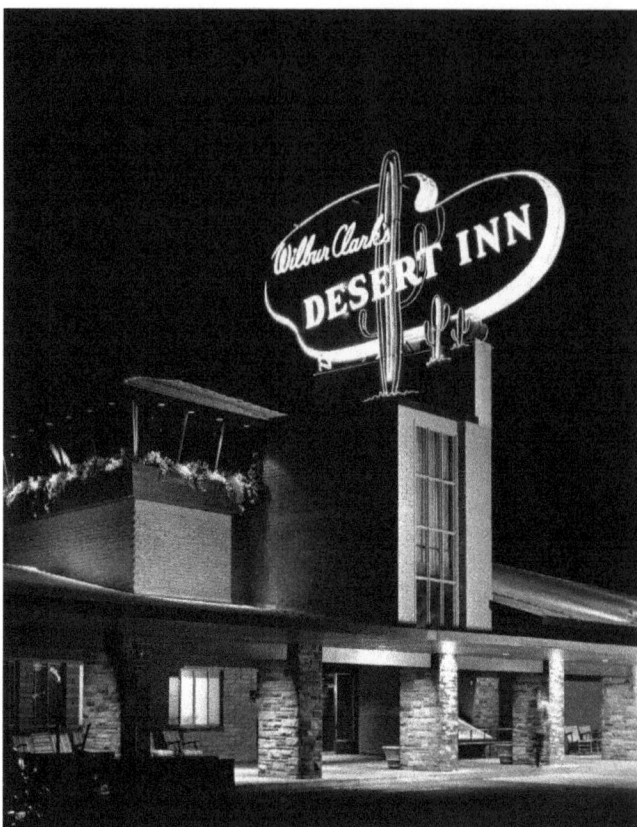

Wilbur Clark's Desert Inn opened in 1950. Two years later, a golf course was built behind the hotel. In 1953, the course hosted a P.G.A. golf tournament called "The Tournament of Champions." Like Las Vegas, it was quite unique. To qualify for the tournament, a golfer had to win a championship that year. That's how the name "Tournament of Champions" came to be. The tournament lasted from 1953 to 1966 at the Desert Inn. The golfers were not the only attractions; many of the showroom stars mingled with the crowds. Each year, a beautiful woman was named "Tournament of Champions Queen." In 1957, that woman was the fabulous Mamie Van Doren. Little did I know that many years later, we would become the best of friends. I attended most of the tournaments and walked alongside my favorite players. At the end of the tournament, the winner was paid in silver dollars.

There was a movie theater on Paradise Road called the Cinerama. It had rocking seats and a big screen. It was way ahead of its time. Today they would call it an I.M.A.X. theater. The last movie I saw there was the 1966 classic called "Grand Prix." The last movie I saw at the Huntridge was "Woodstock" in 1970. I cannot remember the last movies I saw at the El Portal or the Fremont, but I think they were the "Sound Of Music" and "Von Ryan's Express." Downtown had a Woolworth's store, where we used to sit at the counter and drink milkshakes. We shopped at Ronzoni's when we needed clothes and ate at the Sahara coffee shop when we had extra money. We watched gunfights at the Last Frontier Village and attended rodeos at Cashman Field. In those days, gas stations were called service stations. The attendants checked your oil, your tire pressure and cleaned the windshield. One such place was Bob Campbell's Union 76 Station on the corner of Rancho and Washington. Even though we purchased our cars from Community Chevrolet, Bob Campbell did the service on them. Free road maps were also available in his office.

At about the same time, Moe Dalitz, Ben Goffstein, Joe Rosenburg, and Dave Burman were household words. I heard their names so often around the dinner table that I assumed they were just friends of my parents. I didn't realize that they actually ran a lot of the hotels in Las Vegas. In those years, Las Vegas was a safe place to live. People kept their business to themselves. The locals were happy to make a living, and the hotel owners were approachable. In fact, Wilbur Clark would walk through the Desert Inn casino and talk to the employees on a daily basis. Las Vegas was a tight-knit community until 1967, when Howard Hughes bought the Desert Inn. The corporate structure had arrived, and everything changed.

Our address was 1227 Smoke Tree Avenue, and the purchase price of our home was $12,500 dollars. In 1955, the newly built Twin Lakes community was a middle-class neighborhood. Our house was beautiful, but mom wasn't satisfied. She quickly painted it red with white trim. I thought it looked like a barn. Mom was a hard worker. She did most of the painting, but I helped a little. There were no automatic sprinkler systems in those days, so we watered the grass by hand. The yards were large and required a lot of care, but mom and I handled it. Dad wasn't much for yard work. Automatic clothes dryers were not available, or maybe they were just too expensive. Either way, we didn't have one. We had a clothesline. We also had a party line, which meant that other people had access to our telephone conversations. Our original phone number started with the prefix "Dudley." It was later changed to "Orchard." Each time we picked up the telephone to make a call, we had to make sure that nobody else was on the line. We also had to wait until they were finished before we could make our own call. Everyone seemed to handle the situation with courtesy. They had no choice. We also had a milkman, probably from Anderson Dairy. The dairy provided each home with a square box that sat near the front door. We had an ongoing order for certain days of the week. If we wanted extra items, we would simply place our order by leaving a note in the box. The milkman would read the note and leave the order. It was very convenient. I think they billed us monthly.

From the beginning of their marriage, my parents owned their own cars. Dad drove a 1951 Studebaker, and mom had a 1957 Chevrolet Bel Air. I liked the Chevy, but the Studebaker was unsightly. It looked like it was coming and going at the same time. It had large spotlights on each side, so Johnny and I would shine them into the neighbor's living room windows at night. I'm sure the neighbors appreciated that. We traveled to California a lot and always took the Chevrolet Bel Air. Like most other travelers, we would drape a water bag over the hood ornament on the front of the car. It was not for looks. It was there in case the engine overheated on the Baker Grade. They don't refer to it by that name anymore, but it is the steep section of highway around Baker, California. On hot summer days, most cars would overheat. The people who were smart drove at night when the desert was cooler. If your car overheated, you had to pour water into the radiator to cool it down. It never failed; many people were parked on the side of the road with the hood of their cars propped open.

In 1958, I received a genuine Lionel electric train. That was a pretty spectacular moment for a ten-year-old. Another time, I received an electric football game. It was a very simple game. All you did was line up the men and turn on the switch. The field vibrated and made the men go forward. Some went straight, while others turned in circles. It was fun either way.

One of my best childhood activities was playing with a small plastic toy called a Wiffle Ball. It was hollow, light-weight, and had holes on one side. It was actually a plastic baseball. Because of the holes, the ball would curve a great deal when the pitcher released it. Johnny, Mike, and I would play Wiffle Ball for hours at a time. We used a wooden bat, so the ball didn't go very far. Thus, nobody's house was in danger of a broken window. We played in the middle of the street and hit the ball onto the nearby yards. We did the same thing with plastic golf balls. I can remember hitting the balls from yard to yard, using trees for flag sticks. There were a lot of great yards on our street, so we were able to play eighteen holes. As a result, my golf game was pretty good. My prized possession was a real Schwinn bicycle. I wanted to spruce it up, so I took a few playing cards and attached them to the frame with clothes pins. They flapped against the spokes as the wheels turned and made a noise like a small motor. It was the latest thing in the neighborhood. All the kids who had a bike were doing it. Being a young man who enjoyed life, I went a step further. I raised the handlebars a few inches. My bike not only sounded good, but it looked good. In those days, most kids also carried a rabbit's foot key chain for good luck. They came in different colors and weren't very expensive. They were real rabbit's feet. I haven't seen one in years, and I doubt that people would carry them anyway. The P.E.T.A. society probably got involved and deemed it inhumane to possess one. Those were also the days when fur coats were very fashionable. My mom wore mink, beaver, and fox coats when she stepped out on the town. I thought she looked great.

My first introduction to baseball was about 1959. I tried out for a neighborhood Little League team sponsored by Jack's Barbershop. It was a real barbershop in Twin Lakes Plaza. There was an old sandlot where the team gathered. It was an official city league team and very prestigious. Somehow I made the team, but they made me a shortstop. I really didn't like playing that position, but I was a good boy and did what I was told. Soon after that, I became a center fielder. It was there that I excelled. Over the years, I played for many teams, some better than others. I truly loved baseball.

All of the televisions in our neighborhood were black and white, and we felt lucky to have one. If I remember right, ours was made by either R.C.A. or Magnavox. The T.V.s also needed a set of rabbit ears, which was the antenna. The reception wasn't very good. It seemed fine for one channel but not the rest. We had to move it each time we changed stations. After a while, one of our neighbors bought a color T.V. I remember going to his house on Sundays to watch "Walt Disney's Wonderful World of Color." I couldn't believe what I was seeing; the color was so vivid. My friend Johnny Cutler lived across the street at 1224 Smoke Tree. His parents bought something called a Hi-Fi Stereo. It was a huge wooden cabinet that took up most of the living room. The contraption was about three feet tall and eight feet long. Inside, there was a record player, a set of speakers, and plenty of room for storage. When we moved in 1963, my family bought something similar, but ours was even bigger. It had a reel-to-reel tape recorder in it.

While living on Smoke Tree, I had a twenty-gallon freshwater fish tank. I liked tropical fish and had good luck breeding them. I raised Black Mollies, Marble Mollies, Red Sword Tails, and Guppies. They were all livebearers, which meant that the females had their babies live. There were no eggs involved. My secret was to keep the water at the right temperature, feed the fish well and keep the glass clean. One time, a funny situation happened. I can say it was funny now, but I was devastated at the time. My prized Sword-Tail had babies. I was very proud because they were the hardest to breed. I took the tiny fish out of the tank and put them in a bowl on the floor. I had to separate them from the other fish until they grew larger because the adults would eat them. One night my boxer was thirsty and drank all the water. She didn't realize that the babies were in the bowl. It was a sad time for me. After that, I bought a floating device that was made for that kind of situation. It kept the babies in the tank but away from the other fish.

My friend Johnny would take advantage of the warm summer nights in Las Vegas by sleeping under the stars. He slept on a lounge chair in his backyard every night from June until September. Sometimes it was only for a few hours, but he did it anyway. Once in a while, I joined him. It didn't take long for me to figure out his system. When the sun came up, he went inside. It became too hot to sleep. The summer nights were actually very relaxing. We would just talk and count the stars. In the backyard, there were no distractions, like televisions or stereos. I probably wouldn't do it now. I would rather use my Marriott rewards card.

In my early days, ant farms were popular with kids. They were thin, plastic containers that were filled with sand. All you had to do was catch some ants. Well, the ant farms weren't good enough for Johnny and me. We made our own farms out of large pickle jars. We would fill them up with sand and put ants inside. Then, we would add a few sugar cubes. From there, the ants would start digging tunnels. They made themselves right at home. Our glass jars were much better than the kind in the store. The ants had more room to build communities. We collected black and red ants but never mixed the two species. They would fight to the death. To capture them, we would simply hold a small twig to the ground, and they would crawl up on it. From there, we would put them in the jar. As I look back, we didn't need much to entertain ourselves in 1958. Life was pretty simple for ten-year-old kids. Other things that I enjoyed were licorice popsicles, model airplanes, and the monkey bars at Twin Lakes Elementary School. The school had an enormous playground, and I spent many hours there. In those days, the neighbors were friendly. Twin Lakes was not a gated community, nor did anyone pay association fees. There was no need for either.

About 1960, there was a trampoline craze in Las Vegas. Trampolines were actually installed in the ground at the sandlot in the Twin Lakes shopping center. I tried it a few times, but I didn't enjoy it that much. Besides, if you fell and missed, you were in trouble. You bounced right on the ground. I think the craze lasted a few months at the most.

On Saturday afternoons, Johnny and I used to go to the movies in downtown Las Vegas. At that time, the only movie theaters in the area were the Fremont and the El Portal. There might have been a couple of others named the Palace or the Guild. I can barely remember. Everyone's favorite was the Huntridge Theater, but it was so far away that I didn't go there as much as I would have liked. After the movie, we would walk to the Circus Room, a little snack joint across the street from the El Cortez. It only served hotdogs, and you had to stand up to eat. It also had pinball machines, but I was afraid to play them. They were reserved for the tough kids.

One of the great secrets of my childhood was how to build the world's greatest paper airplane. Most boys at that time had their own version of the perfect plane, but I'm proud to say that ours was by far the best. Johnny and I shared the most treasured secret in town, the proper way to build a paper airplane. It was a formula handed down from Johnny's older brothers. It required a series of folds on the right kind of paper. It was a super plane and would fly for a long time. In fact, one night, I took a plane to the top floor of the Sahara hotel and let it go. It flew so far that I didn't see it land. It just disappeared into the darkness. The paper airplane formula was one of the great joys of my childhood, and the price was right.

Every house in our neighborhood had white rocks on the roof. At that time, I didn't think they had a purpose. I just figured everyone had them, so that's the way it was. To this day, Mike Cortney and I laugh about them. Mike is a home builder, and he says that they were probably for insulation. They actually looked great when the houses were new. In 1955 the houses in Las Vegas were pretty simple, much like the town.

I keep talking about the neighborhood where I grew up because my childhood was filled with so many good experiences. There was a small shopping center within walking distance from my house. I would take my allowance to the drugstore and buy candy, especially black licorice. There was also an A&W Root Beer stand. In fact, my first job was washing the big, frosty root beer mugs that A&W was famous for. They paid me a dollar an hour. I eventually learned how to make root beer. I just poured water, syrup, and sugar into a large vat and mixed it up. It wasn't very difficult.

Las Vegas was a 24-hour town, so the people in our neighborhood who worked nights slept during the day. They attached signs on the front door that read "Day Sleeper." They also put tin foil on their bedroom windows to keep the light out. It was very effective. The rooms were totally dark. Now that I look back, it must have been an interesting sight. It was also a quiet place to live. The kids tried not to make too much noise out of respect for the neighbors.

There was also a period when people collected green stamps. As we purchased items from a grocery store, we were rewarded with postage-size green stamps. The more we bought, the more stamps we were given. We would take them home and paste them into small stamp books. I didn't mind licking a few at a time, but I used a wet sponge for large quantities. My tongue could only take so much. After we had enough to qualify for a gift, we would take the stamp books to the redemption center. Being raised Catholic, I thought we would receive preferential treatment because of the word redemption. But we didn't. The center was located on East Charleston Boulevard, a long way from Heaven. I remember picking out a toaster one time and a blender another time. My mom collected green stamps and blue chip stamps, but I think the green stamps were more popular. The modern reward system used by grocery stores is nothing new. It has just taken on a different form.

As a kid, I loved cold cereal in the morning. Some of the brands had prizes inside the box. The one prize I remember most was a frogman, about two inches tall. He was really a scuba diver, but in those days, he was called a frogman. I would put baking soda in his flipper and let him sink to the bottom of a glass of water. In a few minutes, he would float back to the surface. There were also many promotions that were more complicated. Once, I had to send in two cereal box tops. A few weeks later, I received a ring that looked like Snap, Crackle, or Pop. Such was life as a child in the 1950s.

Another story worth mentioning is about a kite, the kind that was available at any drugstore. It was just a couple of sticks and some paper with a picture of the Man in the Moon on it. Being a master kite flyer, I would shred an old rag into several pieces and tie them together. Then, I would attach them to the bottom of the kite for stability. It made the kite look as if it had a tail. Johnny and I decided that we were going to fly this particular kite into the stratosphere. Johnny's dad worked at Nevada Laundry and Dry Cleaning, and he parked the laundry truck at his house. We knew that inside the truck was the largest ball of string in Las Vegas. We needed that string to launch the kite toward the heavens, so we took it. One day the wind was perfect for the lift-off. We attached the string to the kite and let it fly. It sailed over the shopping center and headed toward downtown. The farther it went, the higher it flew. After a while, we could hardly see it. It was soon past the point of no return. We knew that reeling it back to earth was impossible, so we made the exasperating decision to let it go. I would like to think of it as space junk, but it probably landed in some poor soul's front yard.

Johnny and I enjoyed horror movies. In 1959, the theaters in downtown Las Vegas were showing features such as "House on Haunted Hill" and "The Tingler." The scary movies in those days were corny, but people loved them. Some of the theaters had vibrating seats or skeletons swinging from the ceiling. Johnny was ten, and I was eleven, so we were very impressionable. We actually liked getting scared to death. After seeing "The Tingler," we missed our ride home. We had to walk from Fremont Street to Twin Lakes after dark. We walked through the Bonanza underpass and down the Tonopah Highway. I was so frightened that I could hardly put one foot in front of the other. Somehow, we made it home alive. Another time, Johnny's older brother told us ghost stories late into the evening. His scare tactics really worked on me. I was afraid to walk across the street by myself, so my mom met me halfway and escorted me home.

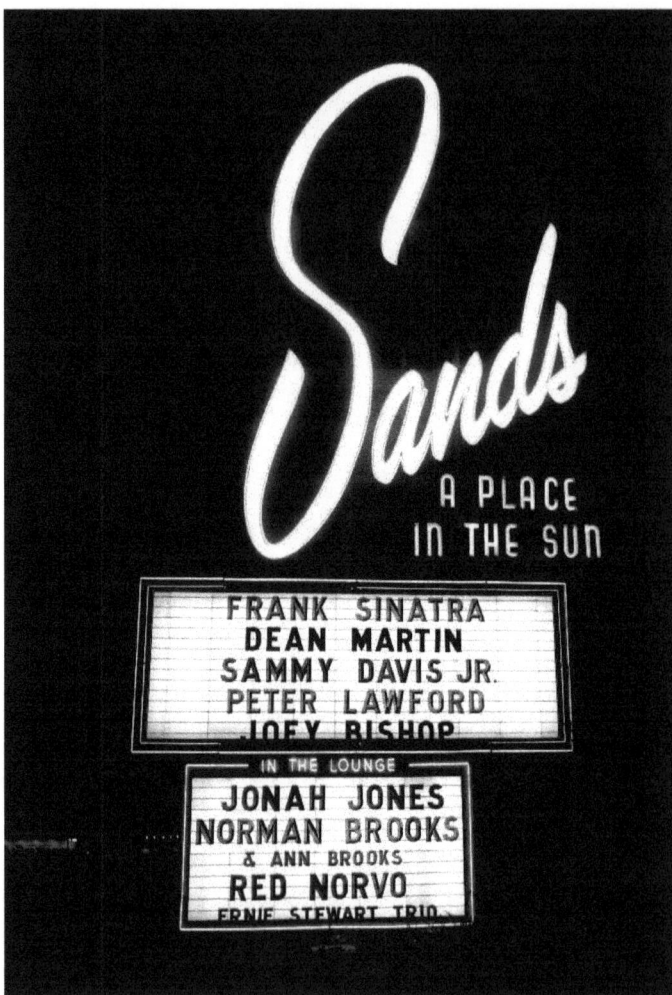

Some of my parent's friends worked at the Sands Hotel. It was the class of the Strip, with great entertainment, good food, and friendly employees. Like the other hotels, its marquee was the centerpiece. In 44 years, the hotel had many different names on the sign, but in January of 1960, the neon marquee displayed the biggest names in show business. Frank Sinatra, Dean Martin, Sammy Davis Jr., Peter Lawford, and Joey Bishop were in town filming a movie called "Ocean's 11." When not working on the set, they would appear in the Sands Copa Room. They gathered on stage in all their glory, with all their egos, looks, and talent. They didn't use a script or backup singers, and they weren't politically correct. They smoked cigarettes, drank whiskey, and did things their way. Frank Sinatra was the most sought-after entertainer in the world. Dean Martin had the best voice of all time. Sammy Davis Jr. was so talented that no stage was big enough. Joey Bishop used his deadpan humor to deliver punch lines that fit every occasion, and Peter Lawford complimented the group the class of a show business veteran. Together they formed a free-wheeling, fun-loving group of guys called "The Rat Pack." Later in life, I met two members of the Pack. It was thrilling.

During my years at Saint Joseph Catholic School, I discovered that all the students had one thing in common, the fear of Nuns. It was worse than the fear of God. After all, the Nuns would hit you; God wouldn't. The combination of their black and white garments and their intimidating looks made us all sit up and take notice. We knew their threats of punishment would be carried out in a swift and humiliating manner. The kids who got caught cheating or talking in class would have to sit on their hands with their knuckles turned downward. This was a form of torture, where their knuckles would become sore from prolonged contact with the wooden chair. Another form of punishment from the Sisters of Saint

Dominic was the hitting of the hands with a steel ruler. This was the most visual and my personal favorite. It was the one that captured the attention of the entire class. There were usually two noises related to this punishment. The first was the sound of the ruler smacking the victim's hands, and the other was the gasping of the students. Although I sat on my hands a few times, I was never the recipient of the steel ruler. I was scared to death and needed my hands to play baseball. I don't know whether it was fear, respect, or manners. Whatever it was, I learned it at Saint Joseph.

Once a year, Saint Joseph would have a unique fundraiser. It wasn't a bake sale or a car wash. It was a Pagan Baby sale. Each student was asked to buy a Pagan Baby for five dollars. I don't remember whether we had to bring the five dollars all at once or whether we were allowed to make payments. Either way, we were highly encouraged to purchase at least one a year. Pagan Babies were young, non-baptized souls from faraway places. Each came with a certificate of authenticity. Over the years, I bought four. After that, I worried about future child support and quit buying Pagan Babies.

When I attended St. Joe's, one of my classmates entered the Soap Box Derby. I didn't know much about the event, so I went to his house and watched him build his car. As he prepared for the race, he told me some of the details. Once I realized that he was going to speed down Bonanza Road in a homemade car, I decided never to enter the race myself. I had no interest in racing down a street that looked like it belonged in San Francisco. I don't know if they race soap box cars in Las Vegas anymore, but I still think about them when I see that portion of Bonanza Road. That event in the 1950s was my first introduction to the sport of car racing.

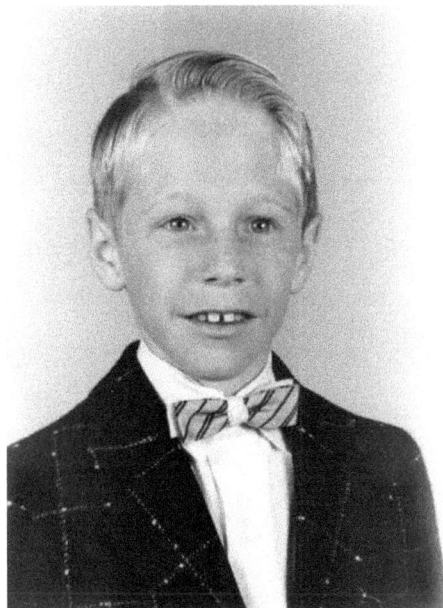

My favorite school teacher was Sister Joseph Anthony. She was a teacher at Saint Joseph, and she treated the students kindly. She also loved baseball. She formed a school softball team, and I joined. I don't remember how many games we played or whether we won more than we lost. I do remember that we challenged our cross-town rivals, Saint Anne, to a game. We were pretty good, but we had no pitching. Guess who was recruited to pitch in the big game? It was me, a natural outfielder. I must have been the only one who could throw the ball over the plate. On the day of the game, we felt great because it was on our home turf. We took the field, and I began pitching. Well, our joyful feelings didn't last long. The boys from Saint Anne Catholic School began hitting home run after home run. It looked like a home run derby. Our strategy backfired. The home field was definitely not an advantage. The left field fence was too close, and they took advantage of that. It wasn't entirely my fault. Nobody else could pitch, either. We took a terrible beating that day, and I never pitched again.

The students at Saint Joe's were required to wear uniforms. The boys wore khaki shirts and pants, while the girls wore plaid skirts and white blouses. At Gorman, only the girls had uniforms, but the boys still had a dress code. It was a good lesson for young people to take pride in their appearance. It was a form of discipline and self-respect. On Friday mornings during Lent, we attended Mass at the original St. Anne's Church. We then walked to St. Joe's in groups. We were allowed to be late for school because it was such a long walk. It was good to be Catholic. I also formed great friendships. Patty Hirsch, Michele Borsack, Jim Olson, and Sonny DaMarto remained lifelong friends.

When I was a teenager, my mom taught me how to drive a car. There was no such thing as driving school, so we did things our own way. We used my dad's 1960 Volkswagen. It had a stick shift and a sunroof. We would go to the neighborhood of Michael Way and Vegas Drive. The streets in that area of town were like country roads. They had very little traffic, so it was a good place to learn. For my lesson, mom and I would switch places, and away we went. I'm glad I learned to drive a car with a manual transmission. It still comes in handy once in a while. I taught Heather how to drive on the same streets but with a different kind of car. I used the same method mom used with me. We just switched places and took off. Heather learned quickly. These days, there is so much traffic in Las Vegas that the last thing you want to do is have an inexperienced driver on the road. I guess that's why they have driving schools.

I did most of the things that the local teens did. I would cruise up and down Fremont Street on weekends, although never in my own car. I didn't have one. I was usually in Bill Sequeira's Corvette or Richie Baez's Oldsmobile Cutlass 442. We didn't cruise during the week because we all had strict parents. Besides, there were no other teenagers on the streets. Every car that cruised on Fremont Street had to turn around at the Union Pacific Railroad Station. At the opposite end of the route was a drive-in called the Blue Onion. The drivers who made the turn there had a long cruise, but most people actually did it. The Blue Onion was a true 1960s drive-in with car-hop service. It was located at the intersection of Fremont Street, Charleston Boulevard, and Boulder Highway. It was strange that all three roads met at one place, but that's the way the city was designed. I never spent much time at the Blue Onion. It was too far from where I lived. I didn't cruise all that much, either. To me, it was kind of boring. I spent most of my free time in my own neighborhood or at the municipal golf course.

Most people my age remember where they were the moment they heard that President John Kennedy was assassinated. On November 22, 1963, I was in Bill Scoble's American History class at Bishop Gorman. As soon as they announced the news to the students, classes were canceled for the rest of the day. That night, I watched the television news in disbelief. The entire country was in shock. The age of innocence was over.

During my high school years, we would go to the Sahara Hotel's coffee shop for a hot fudge sundae or a piece of pie. That was the place to take your date. At least it was affordable. If we had a lot of cash to spend, we would go to the Alpine Village for a great German dinner with all the trimmings. That type of evening was usually reserved for a special event, like a Prom or Homecoming. If my parents let me borrow the family car and gave me some money, I thought I was living high on the hog. When I made reservations at the Alpine Village, I realized Las Vegas was my kind of town.

My first golf clubs were a set of hand-me-downs from my dad. They were made by the Walter Hagen golf company. At that time, I thought they were just another set of used clubs. Since then, I have read volumes on the history of golf and realized that I should have kept them. I was a typical kid. Somewhere along the line, I got rid of them. Today, a set of Walter Hagen clubs would look great in my sports room. When I played on the Bishop Gorman golf team, I used PowerBilt clubs. They were my favorite clubs of all time. Currently, I have Mizuno irons and Bobby Jones woods. They are easy to use, and my game is OK.

After we moved from Twin Lakes, my family's address was 2900 Colanthe. Dad must have received a pay raise at work because the house was in a very nice neighborhood. My parents quickly installed a swimming pool in the backyard. Mom had a maid who cleaned once a week, and dad's barber made house calls. They bought two horses, which they kept at a friend's house a few blocks away. I enjoyed the new lifestyle, but there was a price to pay. I was the one who cleaned the pool, pulled the weeds, washed the cars, and cleaned up the manure in the corral. Those were big jobs, but that's where I fit into the family structure. We lived there throughout my high school years. At that time, my parents were very social, and my mom hosted many dinner parties. She taught me how to mix very fancy drinks, and I became a better bartender than when I was young. Mom was a gourmet cook, so everything fit into their social environment. All in all, I was very lucky. I dressed well and attended private school. Even though I was the smallest kid in my class and wore braces, those were good years.

Because our family owned horses, I went riding quite often. From our neighborhood, it was a short ride to the railroad tracks near the Charleston Underpass. My friends and I would pick up flares, put them in our saddle bags and bring them back to my house. One time, we were chased out of the area by employees of the Union Pacific Railroad. We were frightened, so we never went back. Another time, I was riding through the desert, and a girl on horseback appeared. She was very brash and wanted to race her horse against mine. We did, and she won. Afterward, she told me that she had a much better horse because she was Major Riddle's daughter and could afford a good horse. She also let me know that Major Riddle owned the Thunderbird hotel. I wasn't impressed, just humiliated. It was an interesting lesson.

At one time, Vegas Vic actually talked. The neon cowboy that sat on top of the Pioneer Club was mechanical. He would say "Howdy Partner" every few minutes and wave his arm. Some years ago, he went silent, and his arm quit waving. I photographed the event. A construction crew cut him in half and lowered him a few feet, so he would fit under the new Fremont Street canopy. They put him back together, and he looked fine, but he never said another word. The Pioneer Club is now a souvenir shop.

In the early years of atomic bomb testing in Nevada, we used to watch the blast from our front yards. Since ground zero was only one hundred miles from Las Vegas, we could see the flash of light in the distance. The local media notified the residents when it would happen; usually, it was very early in the morning. As years went by, the above-ground blasts were replaced with underground tests. There were no longer flashes of light, but the ground shook just the same. The hanging lamps would swing back and forth in our house. I was amazed by the idea of the whole thing. As elementary school students, we were told to hide under our desks and that we would be safe. That was an interesting concept. The wind at the Test Site usually blew from west to east. Therefore, most of the fallout was scattered over Utah. We were spared some of the cancer problems that the people of southern Utah encountered. Hollywood got involved with the tests by making movies about them. One movie, in particular, comes to mind, "The Atomic Kid," starring Mickey Rooney. It was a 1954 comedy about a guy wandering through the desert when an atomic bomb goes off. He ventures into Las Vegas, filled with radiation, and the slot machines empty when he walks past them. Well, I don't know how, but I survived all of that turmoil, as did Mickey Rooney.

I actually had many conversations with Mickey Rooney. One memorable time, we were in his room at the Sahara, and his son had just arrived from California. When he introduced us, I wondered how tall he was because Mickey was so short. I had no idea who the mother was, nor did I ask. Another time, I was with Mickey at the Debbie Reynolds Hotel and overheard him telling another member of the press that Judy Garland was the most talented star of all time. He could be right, but I think he said that because they were in so many movies together. The last time I saw Mickey was at the Desert Inn. He was at a press conference with Juliet Prowse to promote the opening of a production called "Sugar Babies." He was great with the media, although it was Juliet who was larger than life. She was a pure talent, an unbelievable entertainer. I remember my dad talking about her when he worked at the D.I. After I met her, I realized what he was talking about.

August 20, 1964, was a Thursday, but not just any Thursday. It was the day the Beatles would perform in Las

Vegas. The morning air had a certain vibe for those of us who were going to see them in person. On the top of the dresser in my bedroom were two tickets to the event of the century, and I protected them with my life. My parents were friends with Italo Ghelfi, an Italian-American from the San Francisco Bay Area who opened the Golden Gate Hotel in 1955. The former Sal Sagev (Las Vegas spelled backward) was suddenly named after a famous bridge. Anyway, most of the major hotels were purchasing blocks of tickets from the Sahara for giveaways to their V.I.P. customers. My mom asked Italo for tickets, and he responded in a big way. The two concerts were scheduled for 4:00 pm and 9:00 pm. I was lucky enough to receive very good tickets to the early show. They were priced at $4.40 and located on the main floor. Realizing that I was in possession of such a prestigious commodity, I decided to take my best friend, Mike Cortney. We were students at Bishop Gorman High School and, like most teenagers, couldn't wait for the show. The Beatles arrived in Las Vegas at about 1:30 am on the 20th and were rushed to the Sahara Hotel under the cover of darkness. A few hours earlier, they performed at the Cow Palace in San Francisco. Stan Irwin, Vice President of the Sahara Nevada Corporation, had the Sahara host their Las Vegas appearance. The marquee at the Sahara stated, "HOTEL SAHARA PRESENTS THE BEATLES Aug. 20, 4 pm & 9 pm L.V. CONVENTION CENTER." They stayed in a suite at the hotel but played at the convention center. The capacity of the Sahara's Congo Room was only 600, whereas the Rotunda held about 7,500. When the day came, Mike and I arrived at the convention center about an hour before the show and were escorted to our seats. The concert started with a few opening acts, including Jackie DeShannon and the Righteous Brothers. The audience was not kind to the performers. They chanted, "We want the Beatles," and were generally rude and unruly. It was the only time I could remember feeling sorry for entertainers. Soon, the moment everyone waited for had arrived. The Fab Four walked onto the stage. As they began to play, the teenage girls went crazy. They began screaming so loud that nobody, including the Beatles, could hear the music. The girls behind us started pulling our hair and pounding on our backs. The event almost got out of control when some members of the audience began to throw jelly beans at the stage. I could tell by the look on John Lennon's face that he was annoyed with the situation. The performance lasted about 30 minutes. The Beatles started with "Twist and Shout" and ended with "Long Tall Sally." There were ten songs in between. When it was over, Mike and I walked to my car. We drove away with our lives barely intact. Our shirts were torn, our hair was missing, and our ears were ringing, but we realized that we had just witnessed the event of a lifetime.

Two years after the Beatles performed in Las Vegas, a T.V. show called "Where the Action Is," starring Paul Revere and the Raiders, was filmed around the Sahara swimming pool. Several Gorman students excused themselves from class that day to watch the taping. Being a rather curious person, I included myself in the festivities. It was the first time I saw a group lip-synching. I was shocked and disappointed. What a wake-up call for me!

As a teenager, I used to roller skate at the Las Vegas Convention Center. I thought it was great. It gave the local kids something to do with their time. I had a friend who was my partner when it came time for couples-only skating. Her name was Jessica James, but we all called her Jessie. I thought it was pretty neat that an older woman would skate with me; she was one grade ahead of me at school. She was the daughter of Betty Grable and Harry James, and she lived on the Desert Inn Golf Course. She had an older sister named Vicki, who enjoyed cooking. Vicki entered some cooking contests and won. During that time, a lot of entertainers owned homes on the Desert Inn Golf Course or in Rancho Circle. Jessie and Vicki were down-to-earth and very likable.

My class was the tenth graduating class of Bishop Gorman High School. Because of the occasion, the keynote speaker at our graduation was Bishop Thomas Gorman himself. As I remember, it was a bittersweet day. I was happy to move on to my adult life but was sad to leave behind classmates and friends from the last four years, in some cases, from the past twelve years. Most of the kids at Gorman came with me from Saint Joseph or from Saint Anne. Many years later, my daughter also graduated from Bishop Gorman High School. It was another Gorman event that I was proud to attend. Although she attended a Catholic elementary school, Heather didn't know the thrill of owning a Pagan Baby. The rights of ownership were finished by then. I do believe she received a certificate of authenticity for buying a Manatee in Florida.

During my high school years, Bill Cosby was a very young and popular comedian. He recorded a few comedy albums, and I had most of them. Bill appeared at the Riviera with Trini Lopez in 1966. Somehow, I got a couple of tickets and took Mike Cortney to the show. Cosby was the opening act, which meant Trini Lopez was a bigger star. Although we enjoyed the entire show, Bill Cosby was the reason we were there. My favorite Cosby album was called "Why Is There Air?" At that time, it was the funniest thing I had ever heard.

The night the International Hotel opened, I was among the many inquisitive locals who attended the event. My friend Johnny was with me, and we were filled with anticipation. We were celebrity-watching, but I was also looking for a date. As we walked through the casino, I spotted a beautiful girl sitting at a blackjack table. I went up to the table and put my foot on the back of her chair. I then started talking to her. I found out that she was from Los Angeles, and her name was Natalie. I eventually asked her to go out for something to eat. After all, I was twenty-one and had a couple of ten-dollar bills in my wallet. She said she would love to, but she was married. As I looked over my shoulder, I saw Johnny laughing like crazy. In fact, he had tears in his eyes. I sadly told Natalie goodbye and went over to Johnny. I asked him what was so funny. He replied, "Do you know who that girl is?" I said that she was Natalie from L.A. He then told me that she was Natalie Wood, the movie star. Boy, did I feel stupid! The night wasn't a complete bust. After that, I went into the men's room and used the urinal next to George Raft.

Chapter 2: Reno or Bust

Because I grew up in Las Vegas, I never experienced harsh winters. That changed when I attended college in Reno. Once the cold weather settled over the university, it was there to stay. It got colder and colder, and all I had was a pair of cowboy boots and an old corduroy coat. Needless to say, I wasn't prepared for life in northern Nevada. After a few months, my boots were stained, and the coat was worthless, but I didn't care. I looked like everyone else. I managed to survive, but my clothes didn't. In the snow, the school was a very beautiful place. I had a lot of friends, and I was happy.

Reno was cowboy country, but it was the sixties, and San Francisco was the place to be. I wanted to see what all the fuss was about, so I went to Haight-Ashbury in search of hippies. I drove with a friend who actually owned a car. We didn't have very much money, so we stayed in a cheap motel. Somehow, we managed to see a lot of the city. While we were there, I bought a pair of pants that looked like the American flag. They were red, white, and blue and covered with stars and stripes. They looked like something Jimi Hendrix would wear on stage. I thought they were very cool at the time. Looking back, they were quite ridiculous. During that trip, the Zodiac killer was on the loose in the city, and I was sure he would get me while I was sleeping. Needless to say, I didn't sleep very much. When we returned to Reno, I had a sense of relief. The hippie scene was a bit much for me.

During the fall semester of 1966, I joined a fraternity named Sigma Alpha Epsilon. We were challenged to a raft race across Manzanita Lake by a rival fraternity, Sigma Nu. They built a raft and asked us to do the same. On the designated day, we were to row across the lake and back. The first team to finish would be declared the winner. Word got out that they actually built two rafts, and they were going to sink ours. Well, one night, we went to their house and stole one of their rafts. We now had two, and they had one. To make a long story short, we showed up for the race with our original raft. We were saving the other one for the last part of the event. They called it a raft race, but it turned out to be a raft fight. At the start, our guys jumped onto the raft and began to row. The two teams passed each other on the first lap without any problems. On the way back, the Sigma Nu boys jumped onto our raft and started to fight, so Sigma Alpha Epsilon returned the favor. We had some big, burly guys from Las Vegas in our pledge class. Therefore, the conclusion was predictable. As the fight progressed, we brought out the other raft. We launched it into the water and began to move past the fistfights. I was a member of the team on the second raft. With most of the student body watching, we crossed the finish line and won the race. The water was cold and dirty, but it didn't matter. We had done it, and that was that.

During my time in Reno, there were rich traditions among the fraternities. In the SAE house, we had a lot of women's groups. We had a Mother's Club that gathered once a month for a luncheon. We also had a house mother who lived with us in the fraternity house. She not only kept everybody in line but managed the financial business as well. There was a group called the Little Sisters of Minerva. They were female students who helped with our study habits and tried to teach us the social graces that we lacked. I was very fortunate to be part of a great organization like SAE. I made life-long friends and learned the true meaning of honor and loyalty. Guys like Sig Rogich, Denver Dickerson, and Bob Corkern taught me how to be a man, while Marc Ratner left a legacy of humor.

I've witnessed a lot of pranks in my life, so I must mention a couple of my favorites. During my days at the SAE house, many interesting things happened. One dark and stormy night, a few of the brothers were talking about a member of the fraternity whose behavior was not gentlemanly. He was attending a night class, so they decided to pull a prank on him. They took his bed, lamp, and dresser to Manzanita Lake. It was winter, so the tiny lake on campus was frozen. Once there, they set up his bedroom furniture on the lake. It was a very funny sight. I admit that I was a small part of the festivities. When he arrived back at the chapter house, it was business as usual, or so it seemed. He quickly discovered that his room was empty and threw a fit. I think the brothers were hoping he would leave. Somehow, he managed to retrieve his furniture from the lake and put it back in his room. Nobody ever admitted to being in on the prank.

The greatest prank of all time happened a few months later. The pledges who achieved their grade point average were going through initiation. The biggest guy in the group had an attitude problem and needed a dose of humility. The Commander, a senior member of the university boxing team, took charge. He walked to Virginia Street and found a parking meter with twenty minutes remaining on it. He ripped the meter out of the ground and brought it back to the SAE house. When Mike walked in, the pledges were working diligently in the basement. He quickly found the one with the cocky attitude. Without hesitation, the Commander threw the parking meter at him and said, "When this time runs out, so does yours." The kid almost got sick. He was scared to death. The Commander was my roommate, so I tried not to laugh. I knew he was just kidding. The rest of the week, the young student borrowed money to keep the meter running. I don't remember what happened to the parking meter, but I'll never forget the prank.

During my years at the University of Nevada, male students were required to take Army R.O.T.C. Nevada was a land-grant institution, which meant that it received benefits from the Morrill Acts of 1862 and 1890. The Morrill Acts funded educational institutions by granting federally controlled land to states to develop or sell to raise funds to establish and endow land grant colleges. Because of that, I had to dress in my R.O.T.C. uniform and drill on the football field for one hour a week. I didn't really like it, but everyone else did the same thing. The Thursday morning routine was easy for me because I attended Catholic school. I already had the discipline.

One important value of college fraternities in the 1960s was the fact that they had mandatory study sessions for the pledges. Each night during the week, the younger students had a designated classroom on campus where they did their homework. They helped each other and were helped by older students. It was a way of guiding them into good study habits. Maintaining a certain grade point average was important to the fraternities. The University of Nevada was a place of spectacular beauty. It had a lake in the middle of campus, complimented by white swans and weeping willows. The campus was green in the summer and covered with snow in the winter. I felt very fortunate to have attended classes there. The atmosphere in our fraternity house was casual, except on Monday. That was the night we had a formal dinner and a chapter meeting. Every member was required to dress in a coat and tie. During the meeting, we discussed current events and decided who was going to run for political office, which intramural sports we were going to enter, and how we were going to raise money for charity. Members kicked up their heels on weekends, but weeknights were usually very quiet in the fraternity house. The Nevada Alpha Chapter of Sigma Alpha Epsilon has been on the campus of the University of Nevada since 1917, and we tried our best to maintain their standards and traditions. I think we did a good job.

Fraternities teach young men the virtues of honor, loyalty, and friendship. In my case, SAE also offered nutritious meals and a great place to live. They are closely monitored by alumni groups, national offices, and universities. Individuals who break the rules are punished, and sometimes entire chapters are revoked. I feel very fortunate to have made life-long friends during my time in the fraternity.

Chapter 3: The Sahara Years

I always loved my hometown, so after a few wonderful years in Reno, I returned to Las Vegas and began my career. Both of my parents worked in the hotel business, so it seemed natural for me to seek opportunities in the same field. The hotels were the largest employer in the state, and it was easy to find a job. I didn't enjoy gambling, so the casino business was not an option. I did enjoy good food, so I accepted a job in the Room Service Department of the Hotel Sahara. It was a natural fit for me, and I enjoyed it from the beginning.

The Sahara had an enormous kitchen. In the center was a long counter where chef salads and other vegetable dishes were prepared. On one wall was a large rotisserie oven that turned out as many prime ribs that were needed daily. Other parts of the kitchen included the entrances to the coffee shop, House of Lords, and the showroom. In close proximity were the bakery and the employee's dining room. There was also an elevator that led to Don the Beachcomber, which was on the second floor. Don Anderson was the Executive Chef and the Food and Beverage Director. His office was in the middle of it all, with the Room Service Department right next to it. My desk was visible through Don's window, so we saw each other every day. We had a great relationship based on trust and professionalism. The kitchen was a well-designed layout. The only problem was that the entertainers had to walk through it to get to their dressing rooms. They would take the elevators in the main building to a hallway, then pass the shopping promenade and into the kitchen area. At that point, they passed Room Service and walked up a flight of stairs next to the stage. It was quite the hike.

I worked all three shifts and loved having the run of the hotel. I excelled at my job and eventually became Room Service Captain. The entertainer's dressing rooms were my responsibility. Because of the nature of my job, I became familiar with all of the celebrities that appeared there. Some I liked and some I didn't. Many of them befriended me, so I enjoyed going to work each night they were in town.

I have numerous stories regarding entertainers, so I will begin with Sonny and Cher. They appeared in Las Vegas many times, but their popularity didn't peak until television made their names household words. Suddenly, they were the hottest ticket on the Strip, and the Sahara had them. Sonny was a happy person and one of my favorites. He was upbeat and easy to please. Every night, he would walk through the kitchen and talk to the cooks, waiters, and cashiers. His friendliness was so contagious that it became a rallying point for the employees during the turbulence of the dinner rush. When Sonny and Cher were in town, I could feel a sense of pride in the air. Our hotel was old, but our showroom was full. The other showrooms were half empty. As I remember, it was the only time employees would sneak into the showroom during their shifts and sit in the aisles. The room was bursting at the seams. They were the most popular act in the Congo Room, and the numbers proved it. They broke all the existing records. Needless to say, the Sahara showroom was the place to be. They even recorded an album at the Sahara in 1973 entitled "Live in Las Vegas." It was produced by Denis Pregnolato and released in 1974. Denis and Cher's sister Georganne were regular visitors to the dressing room. After a few engagements at the Sahara, Sonny and Cher not only trusted me but also invited me to their house in Los Angeles. With that being said, I will tell a quick story about Cher. In 1973, they appeared at the hotel. Cher had recently released an album entitled "Gypsys, Tramps & Thieves." During the show, she sang a few songs from the album. One of the songs was called "The Way of Love." At one point in their routine, Sonny would be alone on stage while Cher changed costumes. She would then stand on the side of the stage, waiting her turn to sing her new hit song. One night, I was watching the show from between the curtains. Cher came over to me and whispered, "When you meet a boy that you like a lot, and you fall in love, but he loves you not." I thought she was talking to me until I saw the microphone. I suddenly realized she was making her entrance to the stage. I froze in my tracks and hoped the audience didn't see me. After that, I stood in the same spot every night, and Cher sang to me. After all these years, that's still one of my favorite stories. Cher was very charming, but Sonny was a real down-to-earth, regular kind of guy. He was a health nut. He liked raw cashews, diet drinks, and other items the hotel didn't keep in stock. Nobody wanted to go shopping for him, so I did. He was also a gun collector.

One time, I picked up a couple of .44 Auto-Mags for him at a gun shop near the Huntridge Drug Store. They were similar to the ones Clint Eastwood used in the "Dirty Harry" movies. He told me that they would never be fired because they would lose their value. When Sonny and Cher came to the Sahara, the house orchestra took time off. They brought their own band of very talented musicians. Their engagements at the hotel were quite a change from the usual pool of comedians such as Johnny Carson, Don Rickles, Buddy Hackett, and Frank Gorshin. David Brenner usually appeared with them as their opening act. While they were in Las Vegas, Sonny and Cher had a few favorite places to eat. One was Batista's Hole in the Wall, an Italian restaurant next to the original M.G.M. hotel. In the summer of 1974, Debbie and I drove to southern California to visit Sonny or Cher, whoever was home. They had a magnificent house on Carolwood Drive. That afternoon, we pulled up to a large gate, and I identified myself. Then, a voice out of nowhere told us to enter. Shortly after that, Cher drove up in her red sports car. She had just come from a photo shoot for Vogue Magazine and was in her usual friendly mood. We had a quick visit and then said, "Goodbye." I always felt at home with Sonny and Cher. In those days, I kept a camera in my locker at work. One night Bob Dylan came to see the show, as he was a friend of Cher's. Cher told me not to bring the camera backstage because he did not like his picture taken. I was glad she clued me in. Situations never seem to change. To this day, he does not allow photography at his concerts. It must be his hair. One night, Sonny and I were having a conversation in his dressing room, and he started laughing. I asked him what was so funny and he told me a story I'll never forget. It seems he wanted to take a swim before the first show that day. Unaware that the pool closed at six o'clock, he went downstairs and jumped in. Suddenly, a lifeguard blew his whistle and ordered him out of the water. Sonny told him that he worked at the hotel and wouldn't be long. But the lifeguard would have none of it and explained that employees were forbidden to use the swimming pool. Sonny found the incident so amusing that he got out of the water and walked quietly back to his room. It was typical of Sonny. He was a mild-mannered guy with a world-class personality.

On a quiet summer morning, I was working in my backyard. The phone rang, and my mom answered it. The phone call was for me. She said it was Sonny from work. She thought he was one of the waiters at the Sahara. It was actually Sonny Bono calling from Los Angeles. He knew I was looking for something else to do with my life, so he offered me a job. He wanted me to be his house manager. The job consisted of taking care of their houses. I would oversee the gardeners, maids, and cooks. I also had to pick up Chastity from school and take her to the studio for the taping of their television show. It would have been a great job, but I didn't accept it. I was about to get married, and the timing was not favorable. It was a job for a single person. Later in the week, "The Sonny and Cher Show" was on television. I asked my mom to watch it. I told her, "That was Sonny from work." After his singing career was over, Sonny moved to Palm Springs. He became the Mayor and married a wonderful woman named Mary. One day, I called him at home to ask a question about The Desert Inn. He wasn't there, but I talked to Mary. After that, they moved back to the Los Angeles area. Then, Sonny became a congressman. I always thought it would have been fun to visit Washington, D.C., and see him as Congressman Bono. Sometime later, I was walking through the Sahara and ran into Sonny and Mary. He was showing her where he used to work. He introduced us, and we talked for a while. It was really good to see him again. After that, he died in a skiing accident at Lake Tahoe. I was shocked. I felt bitter and selfish. The world lost one of its best citizens. I still miss him. If Sonny Bono joined Rock N' Roll Heaven, I'm sure he'd be the leader of the band.

Tony Bennett is a very classy person. Besides being a world-class singer and Las Vegas headliner, Tony is also a very good artist. He paints under the name "Anthony Benedetto." During his engagements at the Sahara Hotel, he would read my books and give me helpful hints. We spent many hours exchanging artistic values. One night, he asked if he could sketch some of my poems. He was already a well-established artist, and I knew he would do a great job. Of course, I gave him permission. If we published a book together, my writing career would take off like a jet from Nellis Air Force Base. I envisioned him talking about the book on the Tonight Show and both of us making a lot of money. One of us was already rich, but the other one could use the money. After years of waiting for him, it just never happened. I couldn't blame Tony. He had two careers going at the same time. The one great thing he did for me was to write a heartfelt endorsement for my work. It reads like this: "Please, World, open up your minds and hearts to this pure poet, Darrin S. Bush, and feel the love he has to offer you, Tony Bennett." Tony inspired me to live a complete, wholesome, and creative life. He has that effect on people. He is always willing to lend a helping hand. During my daily routine, I made sure there was a bottle of Mumms champagne in his dressing room, just in case he had guests. In reality, he didn't entertain as much as the other headliners. He is a man of quiet dignity. Tony never has a bad word to say about anybody. He is well-dressed and well-spoken. While at the Sahara, he always ended his show the same way. He would sit on a stool and sing the last song without a microphone. His voice carried the entire room.

Joey Heatherton was one of my favorites, and I was one of hers. We hit it off right away. After her first few engagements at the Sahara, she started bringing me gifts. One gift was a sterling silver key chain that was engraved with the words "Love Joey." The other was a solid gold pendant shaped with the letters "Sexy." For her birthday one year, I gave her a handbag that I had purchased from the ladies' store in the hotel. It was pink with the lettering "Joey" engraved on it. One of Joey's traditions was to take the orchestra to dinner at a late-night restaurant on Desert Inn Road called Chateau Vegas. She always included me.

During dinner, she would go around to each table and thank everyone for their support. I thought it was a tremendous show of class on her part. Joey liked to help everybody make a living. During the show, she would bring a member of the audience on stage and sing to him. The camera girls would then approach the stage and take pictures of him with Joey. After the show, they would sell him the photos. Everybody went away happy. One night, Joey asked to use the hotel car, a Lincoln Continental. She wanted to drive down the Strip and see all the marquees with entertainers' names on them. The car was unavailable, so she asked to borrow mine. At that time, I had a rather large Pontiac Star Chief with a fresh paint job. Joey took it and cruised up and down the strip looking at the signs. She had a great time, and I came home with a great story. Joey was a sex symbol with a grand sense of humor. After we had become friends, I told her a story about a bunch of guys in Reno. It was the tale of a flag football team named the Fighting Blue Hens. I not only played on the team but helped organize it. During that season, we made her our Homecoming Queen, even though she was not there. Joey enjoyed the story and thought it was a fun gesture. During that time, I was playing on a baseball team sponsored by Shifty's Bar, located on West Sahara Avenue. I asked her to be our Homecoming Queen again, and she agreed.

This time she was in town. She requested that the team come to the hotel, and we would celebrate. When the night arrived, the players gathered in the Sahara Space Center and waited for Joey. I brought her down from her room to meet everyone. We gave her a team jersey and took some photographs. Joey really got into it. She put the jersey on and jumped onto the guys. They held her above their heads like Cleopatra, and everybody laughed. It was pure magic. She wanted to see a game, but she worked two shows a night. One night a fire broke out in the Sahara's kitchen, which was located directly beneath the entertainer's dressing rooms. I quickly ran to the employee's parking lot and drove my car to the back entrance of the hotel. Then, I went upstairs to the dressing rooms and gathered Joey's furs and Tony Bennett's tuxedos. I put them in the back seat of my Pontiac. The smoke was getting very bad in the area, so I went into the hallway and waited for Joey and Tony to come down from their hotel rooms. When they arrived, I gave Tony the keys to the car and told them about the fire. In case of an emergency evacuation, they would be saved. Fortunately, the fire was soon extinguished by the Fire Department. Tony Bennett and Joey Heatherton appeared together frequently at the Sahara. They were a good team. For me, it was a great time to be working there. I usually went home with an interesting story.

James Darren was another one of my favorite entertainers during my early days at the Sahara. Jimmy, as I called him, was famous for his roles as Moondoggie in the Gidget movies, Officer Jim Corrigan on T.J. Hooker, and Vic Fontaine on Star Trek-Deep Space Nine. He is a talented singer and actor but has really made his living on his looks. Like Joey Heatherton, he is a well-rounded entertainer and great for Las Vegas crowds. He has a sensational personality and complete command of his audience. Jimmy and I became very good friends. He actually tried to teach me how to become sexy. He would unbutton my shirt and change my hairstyle, but of course, it didn't work. I was still me. Like the other showroom stars, Jimmy had the option of staying in the hotel. But Buddy Hackett insisted he stay with him at the Sahara's house on their golf course on Desert Inn Road.

Buddy gave Jimmy his start in Las Vegas, so he usually stayed at the house. After all, Buddy was the boss. They were friends, but I think Buddy enjoyed having Jimmy close because the girls would swoon over him. In the early 70s, streaking was in, meaning it was both shocking and cool to run around naked for a short period of time. One night, Jimmy Darren was singing, and Buddy Hackett streaked across the stage. That was the shocking part. The cool part was supposed to come next. The women in the audience waited in wild anticipation for Jimmy to return the favor. They didn't even leave to use the restroom. But to their disappointment, nothing happened. As I saw the events unfold, I thought to myself, "This is just another night in fabulous Las Vegas."

Dan Rowan and Dick Martin had a television show called "Rowan and Martin's Laugh-In." They were also headliners in the Congo Room at the Sahara. Dan Rowan was very well-spoken, well-dressed, and well-mannered. Dick Martin was relaxed, casual, and likable. Most of the Room Service waiters preferred to take care of Dick because he was so laid back. They were intimidated by Dan's formal mannerisms, so I usually took care of him. It actually worked out for the best because we became quite good friends. He gave me a book called "Plain Speaking" from his personal library. It was a biography of Harry Truman. He also taught me the proper way to serve caviar. I was a simple Room

Service Captain and knew nothing about gourmet food. My job consisted of scheduling waiters and dealing with union contracts. Such delicacies were only on the menu in the House of Lords. To properly serve caviar, you take hard-boiled eggs, separate the whites and yolks, and chop them into small parts. Then, you place the caviar tin on a large platter surrounded by small bowls of chopped egg yolks and whites, lemon wedges, red onions, chives, crème fraiche, and small pieces of toast. It was a big production. The first time I served Dan, I only gave him the tin of caviar. At once, he realized that I was totally ignorant, and we both had a great laugh. He then explained the entire presentation. After that, each time I served him caviar from the House of Lords, he would smile and give me a wink. Dan invited me to his home for a visit. The house was in Bel Air, on the same street as Sonny and Cher's mansion. Dan's house had tennis courts in the backyard and lush grounds. He had two large Chesapeake Bay Retrievers. One of the dogs was so strong that it pushed me out of my chair just because it wanted to get cozy. Another reason the waiters enjoyed going into Dick's hotel room was the fact that his new wife was Dolly Read, a beautiful Playboy Playmate. Rowan and Martin's opening act was usually Norm Crosby. He was a master at pronouncing words incorrectly and completely captured Dan and Dick's attention. They watched his show every night from backstage and couldn't get enough of his humor. The employees loved having Dan Rowan and Dick Martin at the Sahara. They were both terrific people.

Believe it or not, Buddy Hackett was a very deep, emotional person. He wrote a few books of poetry and helped me with some of my own writing. He also gave me advice about the publishing business. I knew Buddy very well because of the many years that he performed at the Sahara. We both put in our time at the hotel during its glory days. Because Buddy was so powerful around the Sahara, it was good to have him on your side. People remember Buddy Hackett as a comedian, but he was also a great storyteller. On stage, he would begin a story, then stop and tell a few jokes. Later in his act, Buddy would pick up where he left off and finish the story. It was a good routine. Buddy's son, Sandy, was in his dressing room quite often. He loved football, as did I. We were both Dallas Cowboys fans, so we hit it off right away. One night Roger Staubach's secretary, Roz Cole, made reservations in the House of Lords. Sandy wanted me to pinch-hit for him, so I went into the gourmet room and welcomed Roz to Las Vegas. Needless to say, Roz and I kept in touch. Debbie and I were then invited to a Cowboys game in Dallas. We happily accepted and attended a Monday Night Football game against the Kansas City Chiefs. All of our Cowboy friends played that night. Roger Staubach, Randy White, Robert Newhouse, Harvey Martin, and Drew Pearson were on the field. If there was a football "Field of Dreams," it happened for us that night.

Johnny Carson was a headliner at the Sahara for about 20 years. He was one of the biggest draws the hotel ever had, but his show was always the same. He never changed it. The showroom waiters and waitresses thought he was pretty boring, but the tourists loved him. Personally, I found him to be reclusive. When he stepped off stage, he had nothing to say. He was a plain vanilla kind of guy, and all he ordered from Room Service were cheeseburgers. He was extremely shy, and his dressing room door was always shut. I didn't become friends with Johnny, although I tried for years. I just couldn't get close to him. I did become friends with his wife, and she made sure that I had access to Johnny whenever I needed it. He was very polite, and for that, I appreciated him. He was certainly a superstar.

My relationship with Phyllis McGuire was much better. She usually appeared with Johnny Carson, but her dressing room was bursting with people, music, laughter, and great conversation. It was a warm and happy place. Her door was always open to me. Phyllis endorsed one of my poetry books and sent me gifts at Christmas. I've been to her Rancho Circle home several times. She hosted News Bureau parties and many charitable events. One night, I was there when she had a party for Tony Bennett. It was a grand affair. I can't say enough about Phyllis. She was a real Las Vegas veteran and very good for the community.

Jerry Lewis and I were like brothers and had a special friendship for more than 40 years. As a youngster, I loved his movies, and I knew all of the characters he played. In the 1970's he became one of the frequent headliners at the Sahara. The first time he ordered Room Service, I insisted on taking care of him personally. I walked into his room and stood face-to-face with a living legend. He could tell by the look on my face that I was a big fan. Something clicked between us, and the friendship began. As time passed, we started having very private conversations. I confided in him about my interest in photography and some of the insecurities in my life. He confided in me about his love for kids, dogs, golf, and photography. We felt very comfortable with each other and talked every night. I began playing jokes on him, and he played them on me. Each night he requested a silex of beef consommé in his dressing room. That was just the opening I needed to get into the act. I would leave a note on the silex stating that the consommé was made for one of the characters in his movies. The note read something like, "This is for Captain Eddie." He played so many characters that this scenario went on for years. Jerry never missed an opportunity to clown around with me. One time, Gene Hackman was in the dressing room. I entered the room, and Jerry got up from the couch and kissed me on the lips.

Another time, he was having a meeting with M.D.A. executives. I entered the room with a very large shrimp bowl. I handed him a pen to sign the check, and he dropped it on the floor. I picked it up, and then he dropped the check. I picked up the check, and he dropped the pen. This routine went on for a couple of minutes as we all burst into laughter. When Heather was born, he sent a dozen red roses to Debbie's hospital room. It was a very classy touch. A few months later, Jerry sat me down on the couch and told me he had six sons. He said that he always wanted a daughter, but it never happened. He then asked if he could be Heather's godfather. Of course, I said yes. After that, he began bringing her gifts from his travels. She especially liked a tiny grass skirt from Hawaii. She wore it around the house all summer. One year, he gave her a hand-made Christmas stocking with her name embroidered on it. Jerry's wife Patti made it for her. We still have it and hang it over the fireplace each Christmas. During the 1978 M.D.A. Labor Day Telethon, Jerry wanted to use 15-month-old Heather on the show. We arrived at the hotel a couple of hours early and met with his family. We then went to the Sahara Space Center and took our places. The show began, and we waited for the cue from Jerry. At the designated time, he told Debbie to bring Heather to the stage. With ninety-five million people watching on television, Debbie handed Heather to Jerry. He did a really cute skit with her. He was the comic, and she was the straight guy. It couldn't have gone better. She never cracked a smile. After a few minutes, he said, "Take my kid," and handed Heather back to Debbie. I was very proud. In fact, I paid someone to stay at my house that night and start the Sony Betamax machine. There was a time when Jerry had to watch his diet, and his wife trusted me to take care of him. She would call me with her wish list, and I made sure that he ate properly. The food at the Sahara was good, but she thought Jerry deserved a more personal touch. Debbie started cooking special things for him. He especially liked her German Chocolate cake. It wasn't on his diet, but it was a well-kept secret. The Sahara had a world-class bakery, but he preferred Debbie's cake. Now that's a compliment. Over the years, Jerry gave me a lot of advice regarding photography. People don't realize that he was one of the best writers, producers, and directors in Hollywood. In small bits and pieces, he gave me his knowledge. Years later, I became a professional photographer because of it.

One warm summer day, Debbie, Heather, and I drove to his home for a visit. It was a mansion on Saint Cloud Road in Bel Air, a beautiful section of Los Angeles. Once inside the private gate, we parked in a large driveway that had stripes like a parking lot. When Patti opened the front door, six dogs ran out to greet us. Before she invited us inside, she told us that there were only five dogs last week. She said he must have brought another one home without telling her.

Jerry was a true clown at heart, and his living room proved it. There were clowns everywhere. It was a sight to behold.

Jerry Lewis was a disciplined person. He would perform two shows a night and play golf during the day. I found it phenomenal that he could get up early in the morning, play golf and take a nap before the first show. He also made himself at home while on the road. His hotel room usually had three sets of golf clubs and a few Nikon cameras. His dressing room was filled with posters from his movies and pictures of his sons. For a few years, Jerry wore a neck brace between shows. All of the falls he took during his movie career finally caught up with him. Seeing him in pain night after night made me feel sad. Another thing that I will always remember about Jerry is the fact that he wore white socks. Whether golf slacks, shorts, or a tuxedo, he always wore white socks. There was a tradition at the Sahara that the entertainers would leave gifts on closing night. Most of the stars gave a bottle of liquor to each member of the orchestra. It was a nice touch. Jerry took it a step further. He gave a case of liquor to everyone in the band. Jerry Lewis was nominated for the Nobel Peace Prize in 1977 because of his efforts to raise money for muscular dystrophy research. That's the Jerry I knew. I spent more time with Jerry Lewis than any other entertainer. It was a real privilege. There were many sides to Jerry Lewis, and I've seen them all. He was truly one of a kind.

Don Rickles treated hotel employees with the utmost respect. Once he read their name tag, he would never forget who they were. He was a great entertainer, and his show changed a little bit every night. Don would come down from his dressing room twenty minutes before the show and hang out in the hotel kitchen. He would insult the waiters, waitresses, and busboys until they were laughing so hard that they couldn't face the customers. It was his way of preparing to go on stage. Then, he entered the showroom from the kitchen door. I thought it was a great way to start the show. When he checked out of the hotel, he sent "Thank You" notes to all of the employees who assisted him during his stay. Don had a personal assistant named Harry Goines. They had been friends for 40 years, and Harry was considered part of the family. Because I spent so much time around Don and Barbara, I got to know Harry quite well. At some point during each show, Don would call Harry to the stage and make him part of the act. In 1970, Don traveled to Yugoslavia to film the movie "Kelly's Heroes." Besides Don Rickles, the main stars were Clint Eastwood, Telly Savalas, and Donald Sutherland. Harry also had a very small part. There is a scene near the beginning of the movie where a meeting was being held in a tent. Don turned to a soldier and said, "Hey Harry, go get yourself a haircut." It happened so quickly that I almost missed it. Don made sure Harry was included in the film. Every entertainer should be as friendly and professional as Don Rickles. He was a pleasure to be around, even though he insulted my mother many times. Mr. Venom was, in reality, Mr. Warmth.

Like the other entertainers, comedienne Totie Fields had to walk up very steep stairs to her dressing room. One night she missed a step and fell all the way to the bottom. I thought she suffered a serious neck injury, but she only broke her leg. Like a real trooper, she said, "The show must go on." She actually took the stage for the midnight show. Nobody believed she could do it.

Frank Gorshin was a good guy. He was the greatest impersonator I've ever seen, light-years ahead of everybody else. Off stage, he had a thing for peanut butter. He had it on everything. I was very amused by his craving. It got to the point where I would automatically bring him peanut butter on the side of whatever he ordered. He was the original Riddler in the Batman television series, but it was his live performances where he really shined. I ran into Frank many years later at the Desert Inn. He starred with Jack Jones in Guys and Dolls. I asked him if he needed some peanut butter, and he really started laughing. He was surprised I remembered.

I met Joey Bishop at the Sahara in the 1970s. He was an interesting character because he never ordered anything specific. He would just say, "Darrin, bring me whatever you think I should eat." At first, I answered, "How can I bring you anything? You may not like it." But I quickly got used to the routine and brought him whatever I felt he should eat. It was a very strange but easy relationship. Joey and his wife Sylvia made me feel special. They always invited me to visit them in Newport Beach. Years later, I took them up on their offer.

When Charo was in town, the hotel buzzed with excitement. She was very outgoing and kindhearted. It wasn't an act; it was her vibrant personality. She was born in Murcia, Spain, and had a genuine appreciation for life. Her sister, Carmen, made her costumes and was a constant figure in the dressing room. Charo was a singer, actress, comedian, and flamenco guitarist. During her years at the Sahara, she was married to bandleader Xavier Cugat. Charo was a great Las Vegas performer because she had the ability to control the audience. The noise and commotion of the dinner and cocktail show never bothered her. She was also a very generous person. Although her husband was a musician, he was also an artist. Charo usually brought some of his paintings and gave them to the Sahara employees as gifts. Cooking was another one of her talents. During her engagements, she would put on a chef's uniform and cook paella in the Space Center for the employees who worked the night shift. Paella is a classic Spanish rice dish made with rice, saffron, vegetables, chicken, and seafood cooked and served in one pan. The employees loved her. Charo became a very good friend and constantly invited Debbie and Heather to the dressing room. People remember her as the Cuchi Cuchi girl, but I think of her as the best flamenco guitarist that I have ever heard.

Nancy Sinatra had a large production show choreographed by her husband, Hugh Lambert. Nancy had a few requests that were different than the other entertainers. Only the Room Service Captain was allowed to serve meals in her room. That was me. She also ordered spinach salad every night. It was not on the Room Service menu, so I had to get the ingredients from the House of Lords. Because it had to be served fresh, I prepared the salad in front of her. She always had a uniformed bodyguard escort her to and from her room. Nancy never tipped for individual meals; she gave a very large tip at the end of her engagement. I liked Nancy Sinatra because of her friendliness toward me.

Jim Nabors was such a sincere person. He was born in Alabama and had a southern accent. He played the lovable gas station attendant Gomer Pyle on The Andy Griffith Show. Jim later starred in Gomer Pyle, U.S.M.C. His Las Vegas act consisted mainly of comedy, but a bigger-than-life baritone voice surprised everyone when he began singing. He actually recorded more than 30 albums. I don't think Jim liked to be alone. His dressing room was always quiet. He usually ate dinner at my desk in the kitchen and talked to the employees.

Joan Rivers had a gutsy and sarcastic routine that kept her audience at attention. I felt that she was the female Don Rickles. She thrived on a Las Vegas stage. As far as food, she was easy to please. Off stage, Joan was pretty down to earth. Each night she would walk through the kitchen, stop and tell Melissa to say hello to the Room Service staff.

David Brenner was really fun to talk to. He was the opening act for Sonny and Cher. At that time, the Sahara liked to pair comedians with singers, so there were no conflicts. David appeared on The Tonight Show many times, and I remembered some of his stories. We often talked about a portion of his routine that mentioned how difficult it was to use the restroom on an airplane. It was my favorite skit, and I constantly told him. David was also fascinated with the mob influence in early Las Vegas. He was a good one.

Las Vegas has always been a place where entertainers go to see other entertainers. While I was still at the Sahara, Lucille Ball was watching the show from one of the booths. She got up, came up over to me, and asked where the bathroom was. I then pointed her in the right direction. When she came back into the showroom, we talked again. She was very outgoing and didn't care about being politically correct. She was also taller than I thought.

In the 1960s and 1970s, dozens of cats lived on the grounds of the Sahara hotel. Security guards on the graveyard shift fed them, but they were very wild and untouchable. One night a cat sneaked into the House of Lords looking for a fish dinner. A well-dressed couple in a booth ordered a filet of Sole. They were about half finished when the cat jumped onto their table. He took a few quick bites and ran away. The hotel made sure that the meal was complimentary, but the waiter was embarrassed. The story quickly spread throughout the kitchen, and the hunt for the cat began. They never found the cat, but the employees had a great laugh.

I played a lot of Little League baseball when I was young. When I got older, I coached a Little League team of my own. I needed $500 dollars for uniforms, so I went to Our Lady of Las Vegas Church and asked them for half of the money. They gave me the $250. Then, I went to the Sahara hotel, and they contributed the other $250. I combined all the money, and the team was officially sponsored by a church and a casino. It was a great combination of saints and sinners. I was very proud of that. We had a good team, and we had a lot of fun. We won nine games and only lost five. Buddy Hackett came to see one of our games. A News Bureau photographer took pictures of him with the team that day.

When I wrote my first book of poetry, I wanted a few celebrity endorsements. Even though I worked in the Food and Beverage Department of the Sahara, I had access to the front desk. Bing Crosby had just stayed at the hotel, so I went behind the registration desk and found his home address. I sent him a rough copy of the book and asked him to endorse it. A few weeks later he sent me a letter which said some great things about my work. I thought it was really something special and appreciated his effort.

During my time at the Hotel Sahara, I learned a lot of life lessons. Jerry Lewis taught me about compassion and how to connect with children. Don Rickles taught me that it was OK to laugh at myself. James Darren instilled in me the desire to be the best version of myself. Buddy Hackett told me to be a straight shooter and a sincere person. Tony Bennett showed me how to pay it forward and give others a chance to catch their own gold ring. Dan Rowan helped me appreciate fine dining. Sonny Bono gave me the courage to keep going and enjoy each day. Finally, Joey Heatherton showed me what class and elegance really looked like. Thanks to the entertainers at the Sahara, my people skills blossomed, and I grew into my own person. It was one of the great experiences of my life.

Chapter 4: Frontier Days

After many years of ownership, the Del Webb Corporation sold the Hotel Sahara. A lot of employees were laid off, including me. A short time later, I accepted a job at the Frontier Hotel in the Casino Marketing Department. The property was owned by Howard Hughes' Summa Corporation, and I was excited about a new chapter in my life. Although I did not work for the Frontier as long as I did the Sahara, I managed to accumulate some great memories.

I wore a lot of different hats at the Frontier. During my time there, I was the Room Service Manager, Assistant Food and Beverage Manager, Executive Slot Host, and Bus Tour Promotions Representative. I was also the unofficial hotel photographer, which meant I attended the casino promotion events. Most of them were golf tournaments or V.I.P. parties, but one was very different. It was a hunting trip to a ranch in Arizona. The hotel rented three large Winnebago Motor Homes for the trip. Because I was always willing to help out, I was elected to drive one of them. I had never driven such a gigantic vehicle and didn't know if I could get it out of the parking lot. To make matters worse, Phil Arce, the hotel president, was on my coach. I was a nervous wreck, but somehow I got through the ordeal. I drove it down the Strip and all the way to Arizona. I was on my best behavior because of all the casino customers in the motor home. They enjoyed cocktails, but I didn't. At the ranch, the patrons were treated to a pheasant hunt. It was the first time that I saw real bird dogs in action. They were amazing. When the hunters shot the birds, the dogs would retrieve them just like in the movies. That day, lunch was a pig, which was cooked underground. Between the hunting, the cocktails, the pig roast, and the joke-telling, everyone had a great time. It was a memorable event and another lucky day for me. The Frontier always did things the right way.

While at the Frontier, I was promoted from Room Service Manager to Assistant Food and Beverage Manager. I was immediately assigned to the late shift. The hours weren't exactly what I wanted, but the fierce pace of the hospitality business slowed considerably. When the other managers went home for the day, I had the run of the hotel. I checked the restaurants to make sure they closed down properly and kept my eyes on the bartenders. I also went behind the front desk to check on V.I.P. arrivals. One night, I ran across the name of a hotel guest who had just arrived. The name on the reservation was Dorothy Lamour. I knew right away who she was. I had seen her in several movies from the 1940s and 1950s. One of her most famous roles was playing the straight guy to Bing Crosby and Bob Hope in "Road to Morocco." Well, about midnight, I was walking through the coffee shop and spotted her sitting alone at one of the tables. I introduced myself, and she invited me to sit down and have coffee. Of course, I took her up on her offer.

We had a long conversation about Las Vegas, her life, and her career. Since I had comp privileges, I extended my services while she was at the hotel. Before I said goodbye, I told Dorothy that my daughter had danced on the Jerry Lewis Telethon and asked her to autograph a Keno ticket. It was the only piece of paper on the table. In the end, I found her to be a very gracious lady with an easy-going personality. That was one night I didn't mind working the late shift.

Lee Greenwood was on the hotel's entertainment schedule. He would pinch hit while Siegfried and Roy were on vacation, usually in December. At that time, I was in charge of the children's Christmas party. Along with other acts, I had Heather's dance studio do a few numbers. Heather even did a solo act. She danced to a song called "Dancing on the Ceiling." The employees' children received bags of goodies and had fun with the clowns. I heard that Caesars Palace had Willie Nelson entertain the kids at their Christmas party. Not to be outdone, I asked Lee Greenwood to do the same. He graciously agreed. When the day came, Lee showed up in a white sweater and blue Levis. He walked on stage and was an instant hit. He wished the kids a Merry Christmas, told a few stories, and sang a few songs. He ended his performance with "God Bless the USA." As usual, he left his audience cheering. I've always liked Lee Greenwood. He played a great saxophone and was once a card dealer in Las Vegas.

I can't forget to mention my relationship with Siegfried and Roy. I was the Room Service Manager; therefore, my crew took care of their dressing room orders. In their case, it was more like a large penthouse suite. It was the best entertainer's area I had ever seen, and I've been in plenty of dressing rooms. Even though they were not on the same celebrity level as Frank Sinatra, Sammy Davis, or Dean Martin, I found them to be very demanding. Anyway, one night, they were scheduled to have a lavish party. I helped bring the food around the side of the building, where a flight of stairs led up to their apartment. While we waited for the show to break, their elephant, Gildah, walked from the back of the hotel and stood right next to me. She started swaying from side to side and almost crushed me against the wall. She was looking me right in the eye. I couldn't move because there was nowhere to go. Soon the big creature took her turn on stage, and I felt relieved. On the same note, their black leopard got loose in the kitchen one night, and everyone scattered. It must have smelled the prime rib. Roy had to come and capture it. He saved the day, and everyone went back to work. We all knew that the leopard was one of their most dangerous animals. I did strike up a friendship with Lynette Chappell, their lead showgirl, and personal assistant. She was the only member of the group who treated me with dignity. It's a funny situation. I spent a lot of hours with Siegfried and Roy. I've been to their house several times and attended many press conferences, yet they never knew my name.

A lot of my fellow Frontier employees appeared as extras on the television show "Crime Story," starring Dennis Farina. It was a cross between "Hunter" and "CSI." It was filmed in Las Vegas, so I signed up at the agency that provided extras for the series. About a week later, I received a phone call to work on the set. The episode was being filmed at McCarran Airport, and I had to be there early in the morning. I quickly found out that the extras were herded around like cattle. Once we got our assignments, we were taken to the wardrobe trailer, where we received our clothes. I was to play a cop, so I was given a police uniform and a lousy haircut. My uniform was too big, so they just pinned it in the back. I didn't care; by then, I was hungry and cranky. After a few hours of sitting around, lunch was served. We had to eat at a designated table, away from the real actors. We were not allowed to talk to them. I was beginning to feel like a low-life and wanted to leave. At about three in the afternoon, I was called for my scene. My partner and I were to arrest a Russian pilot after he landed his MiG fighter at McCarran. On command, we ran and jumped into an old black and white police car. I was the designated driver. All of a sudden, a real Russian jet approached the runway. As it landed, I drove the car toward the plane. When the pilot got out, we arrested him and put him in the police car. I then drove the car away from the camera. That was my big scene. We were free to leave the set at about six o'clock. They paid me sixty-five dollars and gave me a nice firm handshake. As I left, I thought I should have spent the day doing something more productive, like golfing or pulling weeds. I decided at that point that my acting career was over. It was not a pleasant experience. If I wanted to be treated like a second-class citizen, I could have been someone's butler and made more money.

I became very good friends with two acts that appeared in the Frontier's showroom, Paul Revere & the Raiders and The Righteous Brothers. I enjoyed their music for many years and was absolutely thrilled to interact with them on a personal level. Paul Revere's Raiders became my golfing buddies. When the group appeared at the Frontier with the Righteous Brothers, I was in charge of their dressing rooms. Looking back at my life, I have probably spent more time in hotel dressing rooms than anyone, including performers. Anyway, Doug Heath, the lead guitar player, and Carl Driggs, the lead singer, would meet me at the old Muni golf course on the corner of Decatur and Vegas Drive. We could play any day of the week because we all worked at night. We were similar golfers. None of us took it seriously, and we always had fun. Both showroom acts had great personalities. They were constantly playing jokes on each other. Since I have always enjoyed a good joke, they all enjoyed my company. The Raiders and I became such good friends that I was considered an honorary member of the band. We started going to dinner together and sending Christmas cards. One year, I caught up with Paul and the boys at the Governor's Conference on Tourism in Reno. I photographed the show in a huge bowling alley. It was great fun. I loved their songs.

One summer, Paul decided to ride a motorcycle from the Harley Davidson store in Las Vegas to Washington, DC, where he was scheduled to perform on the fourth of July. Again, I was there. After a short press conference, Paul and Omar, his drummer, hopped onto motorcycles and took off. His wife, Sydney, and I said goodbye in the trailer that was to follow them. Paul named the trip "Rolling Thunder," and he picked up other riders along the way. Soon after that, they came out with an album named "Ride to the Wall." It was dedicated to the men and women who served in the Vietnam War. It's a Paul Revere and The Raiders masterpiece.

One night, Bobby Hatfield and Bill Medley put on their sunglasses and swimming suits as if they were coming from the pool. They walked on stage and started harassing Paul and the Raiders during their portion of the show. It was a great prank. Of course, Paul had to get even. So, The Raiders put on "Louie Louie" sweatshirts and harassed the Righteous Brothers during their performance. The Raiders gave me one of the sweatshirts the same night. Since Bobby Hatfield was a fraternity brother, I decided that it was my turn to pull a prank. One night I filled his dressing room with SAE posters, pictures, and coffee mugs. He loved it, and from then on, we were best friends. In all my years of dealing with entertainers, I was closer to Bobby and Bill than anybody. I spent a lot of time with Bobby in Newport Beach. From Righteous Brothers concerts for the Lupus Foundation to having enchiladas in his living room, we always enjoyed each other's company. We played golf at the Newport Beach Country Club and lifted a drink or two at a restaurant called the Quiet Woman. Since Bobby was an SAE, he always gave me the secret fraternity handshake. It was funny because he would turn his back on everyone else, so they could not see it.

Dave Bronson, the Righteous Brothers drummer, had some great parties at his house. Even though it was hard for me to stay awake, I would drive Bobby there and give him a ride back to the hotel. Dave lived two houses away from former Lieutenant Governor Lonnie Hammergren, so it was quite a drive to the Strip.

I remember the night Bill Medley left the Frontier and flew to Los Angeles to shoot the video of "I've Had the Time of My Life" with Jennifer Warnes. They filmed it in the middle of the night in a warehouse in downtown L.A. It became the theme song for the movie "Dirty Dancing." He told me the next night that he was very proud of it, and he knew it would become a hit because of where it was placed in the movie. He was right. Then he gave me a jacket to make me a family member of his own band. The jacket was black with red letters that read "Bill Medley, WT Band, Darrin." The "WT" stood for William Thomas, his proper name. There were only 12 jackets made, and I had one of them. Bill did perform separately from Bobby on occasion.

Bobby Hatfield had the best personality of anybody I've ever known. He and I were always joking about fraternity life, entertainment, and everyday events. I was in Newport Beach on business one day, so I called Bobby. I told him that I was bored, so he invited me to his house. He then told his wife that we were going to the Quiet Woman to have a few drinks. We hopped in his car and went to the QW. It was a great place to eat, but food wasn't on the menu that night. We parked in the back, walked in, and sat at his favorite spot near the end of the bar. Bobby ordered his usual drink, and I had the same thing. I believe it was vodka mixed with orange and pomegranate juice. We told fraternity stories, talked about sports, and solved all the problems of the world. We sipped cocktails for a couple of hours, then got into his car and left the QW. We took side streets back to his house because he didn't want to get stopped by the police. Hanging out in Newport Beach with my dear friend Bobby Hatfield was both fun and relaxing.

I must tell a great story about Bobby. He called me one day and said that he would like to have an article about himself in The Record, the official SAE magazine. I said that I would be glad to interview him, but Mr. Hatfield had a different idea. He wanted to interview himself, and he had specific questions in mind. Bobby went into his bedroom with a cassette recorder and began to talk. You have to understand that he had a sensational sense of humor. Bobby asked himself funny questions and had witty answers. The most interesting thing about the tape was the fact that he used a goofy-sounding voice as the interviewer. In fact, it was so entertaining that he laughed at himself during the taping. Linda came into the bedroom more than once to find out what was going on. Well, after he finished the project, I typed it on Righteous Brothers stationary and sent it to the fraternity headquarters at Northwestern University. When it finally appeared in The Record, it didn't sound very much like the original. It was edited so much that it was rather short and rigid, but it worked out fine. Bobby was happy, and the fraternity was happy. I still have that tape. His lifelong singing partner, Bill Medley, has never heard it.

Like most of the hotels in Las Vegas, the Frontier was ultimately sold, and I was once again out of work. This time, it was different. I was getting older and needed to find a career with more stability than the hotel business.

Chapter 5: Las Vegas News Bureau

In 1988, my next-door neighbor informed me of an opportunity at the Las Vegas News Bureau. One of their photographers retired, and they were looking to fill the position. The News Bureau was established in 1947 by the Chamber of Commerce to promote tourism. I majored in Journalism at college and felt it was time to turn my passion for photography into a career. The idea of promoting my hometown through my photos was very appealing, so I interviewed for the job. My dream came true, and I was hired as a photojournalist. In 1993, the News Bureau was transferred to the Las Vegas Convention & Visitors Authority. I came with it and spent twenty-six years documenting the fabulous history of Las Vegas. The photo assignments at the News Bureau were very interesting, and I enjoyed every minute of my life. The job put me in new situations daily. As a photojournalist, I had the run of the town, and the streets of Las Vegas became my office. I took photos in every hotel and from most of their rooftops. Carrying a camera allowed me entrance to most of the events I wanted to attend. I awakened early in the morning for professional golf tournaments and worked in the middle of the night photographing hotel implosions. I've also had my camera equipment searched by the Secret Service when the President was in town. I attended groundbreaking ceremonies, rock concerts, and boxing matches. During my twenty-six years at the News Bureau, I was sent on seven thousand photo assignments and contributed more than four hundred thousand images to the archives. It was a very fulfilling time in my life.

As far as photo shoots, I've always enjoyed hotel openings. Being a member of the press, I was usually invited into the hotel the day before it opened to the public. I was able to photograph the casino, the restaurants, the rooms, and the pool. Most of the time, the openings were quite festive. There were fireworks, and all the restaurants served food. There were some good openings and some that were not so good. New York-New York, Excalibur, and MGM were great fun. They spared no expense on the festivities.

There had been a wall around the MGM Grand property for years that read, "Watch us roar in 94." The opening party was sensational, but I wanted to get a shot of all the people rushing in the front doors the next day. I went to the top of the Excalibur early on the day of the official opening to shoot the mass of humanity. As it turned out, the doors were open all night, and nobody rushed through the lion's mouth. Some things just don't work out the way you envision them. Eventually, the hotel changed the front architecture, and people could no longer walk through the mouth.

The Luxor was one of the best openings because they pulled out all the stops. There were people dressed in costumes from ancient Egypt. There were strolling musicians and a lot of great photo opportunities. The first show at the Luxor was called "Winds of the Gods," an Egyptian production show. The choreography, dancing, and costumes were very colorful. It was a memorable occasion for me, but I had a feeling that nobody else would remember it. Hopefully, people will always remember the Folies Bergere at the Tropicana. Too much Las Vegas history has slipped through the cracks.

The Stratosphere was one of the worst openings. Too many people were packed into small areas, and there wasn't much food. I left early and went to the top of the Sahara parking garage to shoot the fireworks. The Wynn opening seemed strange to me. There was no press event or formal opening. They had a private dinner for VIPs, but that's all. The press was not allowed on the property. The Bellagio opened the same way, as did Encore. I guess that's just the way Steve Wynn did things.

I photographed the Grateful Dead at Sam Boyd stadium in 1993. It was a very hot day, and I didn't care about the band. To make things worse, their security people weren't very nice. I took a few pictures and left. The only thing that made the day tolerable was the fact that somebody stood up in front of me and held up a Grateful Dead t-shirt. He looked at me, I took the picture, and it turned out to be a classic. That shot told the story more than the singing group.

When I first started shooting boxing, the promoters would give out gifts at press conferences. Some of them were pretty elaborate. At first, members of the press received sweatshirts, then it was t-shirts, and then they handed out commemorative coins. Finally, it was just food coupons at a concession stand. Most of the time, they did have an elaborate food spread in the press room during the fight. If the match was between two Mexican fighters, they served Mexican food. If the boxers were American, the spread was different. I enjoyed shooting boxing because it was so exciting.

I especially loved photographing title fights because everything was on the line. The Riddick Bowe vs. Evander Holyfield fight at Caesars Palace was one such match. The atmosphere was electrifying. Most heavyweight title fights are like that. I appreciated seeing athletes in their prime. I think they fought twice, with each one taking a victory. A year or so later, I attended one of the greatest fights of all time. Evander Holyfield fought Mike Tyson at the MGM Grand Garden. Everybody thought Mike was going to win because he had been released from prison and seemed ready for anything. Well, to everyone's surprise, Holyfield knocked out Tyson. I've never seen anything so thrilling. The audience went crazy. Another good fight was the George Foreman and Michael Moorer match-up. Michael was the heavyweight champion, and George Foreman was well past his prime. During the fight, Foreman looked sloppy and slow. On the scorecards, Moorer won every round. The only way for George to win the fight was to knock out his opponent in the last round. George did just that. He landed one big punch, and Michael went down. The fight was over in the blink of an eye. Needless to say, the people in the arena got their money's worth.

Media credentials can be difficult to obtain. There is a process that the media outlet must go through to access an event. A request is sent to the Publicity Department of the venue host. In Las Vegas, it's usually a hotel. Upon acceptance, a writer or photographer goes into the host office and has an identification photo taken. That photo is printed on the front of the credential, along with the date and name of the event. On the back is an agreement, which states the conditions of the credential. When I shot the Tyson vs. Holyfield fight, my credential stated that it was issued by the MGM Grand and Don King Productions for the sole purpose of providing access to the event for news media. "Any secondary, non-editorial, or commercial use of any pictures is prohibited. Credentials must be worn in plain sight at all times. I understand that this credential provides me with a reserved position from which to watch the fight." At the bottom was my signature. Over the years, I collected a lot of credentials.

Regarding the Mike Tyson and Evander Holyfield fight, it was the best boxing match I've ever seen. In those days, we shot film, and I used black and white for a couple of rounds just to give it that old-time flavor. One frame came out so good that I printed it and decided to have both fighters autograph it. A few months passed, and I finally caught up with Evander Holyfield at a press conference. I took the picture in the room where all the sports writers and photographers had lunch. When the event was over, I approached Evander and asked him to sign the picture. He signed it "Holyfield 3:16." That's the way he signs things. I then needed Mike Tyson's signature. That was a little more difficult. I didn't know when I could catch up with Mike. I knew that he worked out at Fay's Golden Gloves Gym, located behind television channel three in North Las Vegas. I called Fay and explained everything. She said that he would be glad to sign the picture and told me to arrive at the gym on a certain day. When I arrived, Mike was working out in the ring. After a while, he went into the locker room. I followed him shortly after that. Mike was sitting down, taking off his gloves. We had a nice conversation, and then he signed the picture. My mission was complete. Before I left, he asked me for some pictures of his other fights. I said that I would drop them off with Fay. I then left the gym. He did his part, and I did mine. It was a unique experience.

The only other autographed boxing photo I have is from a fight between the German champion Axel Schultz and George Foreman. I shot the fight at the MGM in 1995. Again, I wanted the picture signed. As luck would have it, I caught up with Axel Schultz at the Desert Inn coffee shop one day. He was having lunch with a few of his friends. I took the picture over to him, and he signed it. I thought it would be hard to find him because he's from Germany. But, once again, I was in the right place at the right time. Getting to George Foreman was more difficult, but eventually, he signed the picture. Boxing is the most exciting sporting event I've ever covered. I guess I liked the intensity of it. It can end in the blink of an eye.

I also photographed rodeos. Las Vegas hosted the National Finals Rodeo, which was the largest event on the rodeo tour. It had the best participants and the biggest prize money. There was a small press room with sandwiches inside the Thomas and Mack, but you had to arrive early, or the food was gone. They did not keep it flowing like the boxing events. I enjoyed the NFR, but it was not as much fun as the fights. The photographers were crammed into a small area like sardines, and it was difficult getting in and out. We were right on the rail, so the animals would smash against us from time to time. I didn't care, but the arena smelled like a stable, and that brought back some bad memories. The bulls also covered me with whatever was coming out of their nose. The riders were tough, and the animals were big, so I had to be alert at all times. The sights and sounds of rodeos were exciting, but they were too crowded. When I began to work the day shift, I realized that I did not miss that event.

As a photojournalist, I was escorted in and out of music events. The first two songs were all I was allowed to shoot. Rarely did the hotel people allow me to stay and see the show. One such time was during a Ringo Starr concert at the Rio. The public relations girls from Harrahs allowed me to see Ringo's entire show. It happened again at Caesars. After I photographed Carol King, I put the camera away and watched the rest of her show. She was an outstanding performer. The only thing on stage, besides her, was a piano. After the event, I told everyone involved that it was a nice gesture on the part of Caesars to let me see the performance.

I loved shooting implosions, even though they were late at night. They were usually scheduled in the wee hours; that's when traffic on the Strip was at a minimum. All in all, I photographed ten implosions. The one thing they all had in common was the cloud of debris they created. I called it

Implosion Dust. When a building explodes, an incredible cloud immediately spreads over everything in its path. It goes for blocks, and nothing is safe. I learned to park far away and wear old clothes. As soon as the building hit the ground, I would pack up my camera, unfold the tripod and run to the car. The secret was to stay ahead of the cloud. It would creep along the city streets like fallout from an atomic bomb. My usual routine was to arrive early and stake out my spot. I would then set the camera on a tripod, calculate the correct light reading, and wait for the event. In most cases, it took two hours of waiting to shoot a six-second event. Most of the time, I managed to shoot a dozen frames before the building crumbled into history. When I arrived home, I would take off my clothes and leave them in the garage. I liked implosions because I was able to witness events that changed the face of Las Vegas.

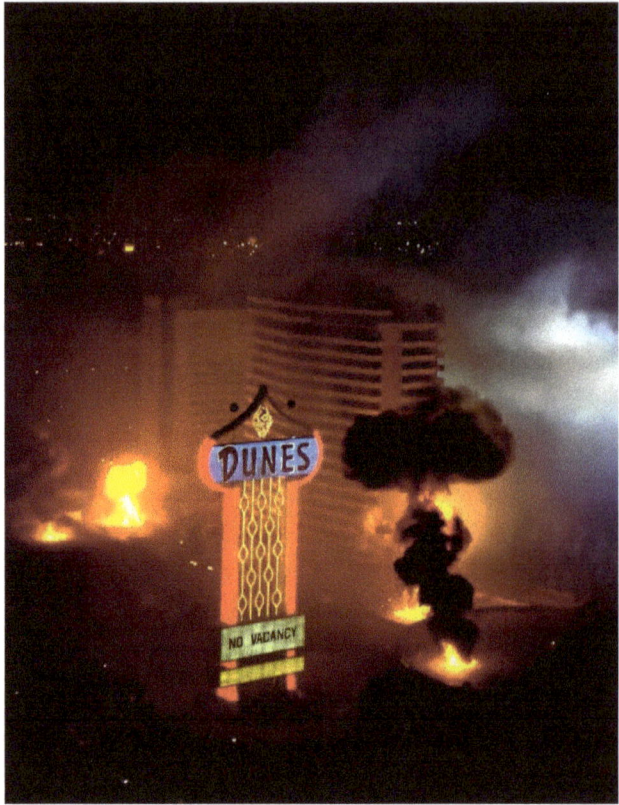

My first was at the Dunes hotel in 1993. I shot it from
the roof of the Barbary Coast parking garage. It was quite a
spectacle because Steve Wynn filmed it for a TV movie
called "Treasure Island." People lined the Strip to watch. I
used two cameras, one with black and white film and the
other one with color film. Because Steve had a flair for
dramatics, there were explosions and fireballs. First, the
famous Dunes marquee fell over, and then the building
caved in. I felt bad for the mice and cockroaches still inside.
I'm sure they didn't feel a thing.

The Dunes actually had two towers. A few months after the first implosion, the second tower was scheduled to be brought down. This time I was ground level, in their parking lot. I was too close to the action, and I knew it. As soon as the tower hit the ground, I ran toward my car. This time, I barely made it. When I closed the door, the cloud covered the car. I had to wait for the air to clear before I was able to drive away. That was a close one.

The worst implosion I photographed was on New Year's Eve, 1996. That's when the Hacienda hotel came down. I waited for hours across the street. That night, the media was mixed in with the general public, which is never a good idea. We were too close to the subject, and there were too many people. We were in harm's way with nowhere to go. Just before the implosion, someone turned out the lights on the building, causing total darkness. It was so dark that I could barely see anything. As the implosion began, I took photos but didn't have time to get out of the way. Suddenly, everything in the area was covered with debris. Dust particles were in my ears and mouth and on my clothes. From then on, I made sure that no part of my body was exposed during implosions. I learned a lot from that event.

The Landmark hotel was my favorite implosion. It was certainly the most visual. Warner Brothers was in the process of filming a movie called "Mars Attacks." Since the Las Vegas Convention Center owned the land on which the

Landmark sat, they had to sign an agreement with Warner Brothers not to use the images of the implosion for one year. That gave the studio the time they needed to release the movie. I think Jack Nicholson was in it. The movie was a spoof on aliens attacking earth. Anyway, I was on top of the Debbie Reynolds hotel for that event. The studio wanted to film it at 5:00 a.m. They wanted to get the glow of the morning sun rising in the background. I remember watching the rehearsals a couple of hours before the actual event. The actors were running down the street, away from the hotel. People were driving cars as if in a panic. When the time came for the real thing, they only had one take to get it right. The implosion was for real. I looked down and saw Lorraine Hunt, Chairperson of the LVCVA Board of Directors, push the plunger. The cameras were rolling, and the actors were running. The sky was glowing orange, and the hotel tumbled down. Afterward, I went to the Hilton for breakfast. I didn't get dirty that morning because I was so high off the ground. I liked implosions, but I always had mixed feelings about them. As a photographer, they were exciting. As a Las Vegas native, it was sad to see the changing of the guard.

Balloon races are not really races. They're more like a game of 'follow the leader' or 'the hare and the hound.' The lead balloon takes off and maneuvers itself along a certain path. The rest of the pack follows as best as they can. In 1995, I was allowed to fly in one of the balloons in Laughlin. The lead balloon took off, did a few turns, and then dipped down toward the Colorado River. It sat on the water and floated a few hundred yards. Our balloon did the same thing. As we skimmed the water, the basket got wet on the bottom. Of course, my shoes were soaked, and I had to wear them for the rest of the day. Thank goodness the air was warm. The flight lasted about an hour. It was quiet and smooth. Since then, I have been on several hot-air balloon flights. The only thing better is a ride in a blimp.

I photographed George Burns on stage and at press conferences. He was an old gentleman in his nineties at the time. I took pictures of him as he signed a contract to play at

Caesars Palace on his one-hundredth birthday. We were all hoping that he would make it, but he didn't. He did live to be one hundred, but he was too fragile to do his show. When he died, Caesars paid respects to the veteran entertainer by placing a message on their marquee. It read "George Burns 1896 to 1996." As usual, I went to the Strip and took pictures of the famous sign. To me, that night wasn't just about another celebrity passing away. It was about a man who lived to be one hundred years old and was under contract to headline in a Las Vegas showroom.

In 1996, the Sands hotel was preparing to close its doors forever. As usual, I drove to the Strip to document the occasion. The last Sands marquee read, "OPENED DECEMBER 15, 1952, CLOSING JUNE 30, 1996, 44 GREAT YEARS, THANK YOU." I took a shot of the sign with the hotel in the background. It was a good shot but a sad occasion. The Sands hotel was a real classic. It represented a very special era in Las Vegas' history. It was the home of the Rat Pack. Weeks later, I went back to the Sands to take pictures of another occasion. Touchstone Pictures was filming the movie "Con Air." This time, there was a large airplane parked by the front doors. It was meant to look as if it had crashed into the building. When I saw the film, the special effects made the crash sequence look real.

While the Dunes hotel was preparing to close, there were several photo opportunities around the property. I was there as the Security Department locked up different parts of the hotel. As they walked through the casino, they shut down the roulette wheel and put tape around the slot machines. When they announced that the last keno game was to be played, I bought a ticket. I wanted to buy the last one, but someone else did. After the game, I asked him for the ticket. He gave it to me, and I donated the ticket to the News Bureau's collection. Somewhere in the vault is the last keno ticket played at the Dunes. The Dunes hotel was unique. It was one of three hotels that had an 18-hole golf course attached to it. The others were the Desert Inn and the Tropicana. I enjoyed the Desert Inn and Dunes courses, but the Tropicana had too many hills for my game. The Dunes had an elegant seafood restaurant called "The Dome of the Sea." For seafood lovers, it was a treat to enjoy a delicious lobster or halibut dinner in such a beautiful restaurant. There was also a winding river and a woman floating on a barge while playing the harp. The Dome of the Sea was the epitome of class and was reserved for very special occasions.

I sent a lot of photos to the Associated Press over the years; some had more significance than others. The opening of the Bellagio generated a great opportunity to showcase Las Vegas. Opening night was windy, so they canceled the fireworks show. Inside, the gala event went on as scheduled. It was by invitation only. Something told me that Steve Wynn would light off the fireworks at some point, so I went back the next night and set up my tripod in front of the hotel. There were very few photographers that night. I took a chance, and it paid off. The fireworks went off at dusk, and they were spectacular. They were launched from Bellagio's lake, and they lit up the entire property. I went back to the office and sent my best picture to AP. That photograph ran all over the world. It was not just the opening of the Bellagio; it was the opening of the most lavish hotel Las Vegas had ever seen. I had pretty good luck sending images to the wire services during my career. The News Bureau was not in the business of competing with local newspapers, but we did get our share of international publicity.

On one assignment, I took my daughter, Heather, and fellow photographer Glenn Pinkerton to the Bellagio. I needed pretty faces and cheap labor. I wanted to shoot people eating lunch at Olives, a restaurant overlooking the lake in front of the hotel. It was a beautiful setting, but the staff did not treat us very well. In fact, they refused to put food on the table. We made the best of it and took the picture anyway. I couldn't send it to AP because it was not a news photo, but I saved it in the archives. A few months later, it showed up in the Chicago Sun Times. The photo took up an entire page in the travel section. You just never know who will use News Bureau pictures.

I've photographed hundreds of press conferences, and each was interesting in its own right. One, in particular, stands out from the rest. During a press conference to promote Spamalot, Steve Wynn actually got up on stage and sang with the cast. The other participants were actor John O'Hurley and producer Eric Idle. They sang "Always Look on the Bright Side of Life." That day, I sent a shot to AP of Mr. O'Hurley jumping out of a can of Spam. That was a good press event, and the picture got a lot of attention.

I've attended many after-show parties on media night. Some of the best were: Barry Manilow at the Las Vegas Hilton, Wayne Newton at the Stardust, Hootie and the

Blowfish at the Silverton, and Kevin Bacon at the Rio. These were fun because the performers mingled with the crowd. There were many more; I just can't remember them.

During the opening of the Debbie Reynolds hotel, a funny situation occurred. Debbie was to appear as the first act in the showroom, but the room was not quite ready for the show. It needed cleaning up. For some reason, Debbie took it upon herself to get the room ready for her performance. An hour before the show, Debbie Reynolds was in her bathrobe, vacuuming the floor. As the doors opened, she told the guests not to mind her. She was killing them with laughter. I never did figure it out. Either the floor was really dirty, or she planned it as a stunt. She always did comedy. This could have been part of the show. Whatever it was, it worked. The curlers in her hair added to the routine. She certainly had me convinced. I've never seen a showroom star vacuum the floor before.

I can't remember why, but I attended a party at Phil Maloof's house in Rancho Bel Air. He was a billionaire, so we didn't have much in common. He lived in a rather large house. In fact, it was so big that it had a Piper Cub airplane in the living room. After socializing for a while, I noticed that Tippi Hedren, Angie Dickenson, and Stella Stevens were at the party. I wanted to take a picture of them, so I placed the three girls on a winding staircase. They posed for me, and I took their picture. Stella Stevens was the friendliest. Years later, I caught up with her at an event at Alexis Park. She was as friendly as ever. All entertainers should be that nice.

One day, I was driving by the Las Vegas Hilton. I looked up and saw Barry Manilow's name on the marquee. It was a large sign, but its predecessor was bigger. It was one of the most impressive signs I've ever seen. Unfortunately, it was demolished during a wind storm in 1994. After the wind blew it down, the current version was constructed. As I think back, I remember several different marquees at the Hilton. The hotel opened in 1969 as the International, and Barbra Streisand was the first name on the marquee. A year later, the property became the Las Vegas Hilton. Over the years, the marquee has publicized many different names, such as Elvis Presley, Nancy Sinatra, Starlight Express, and Alabama. The International also had a large room which they called a "Legitimate Theatre." Its size was somewhere between a showroom and a lounge. I was there once and saw the Broadway play HAIR. It was extremely visual, controversial, and uplifting. It portrayed the hippie culture of the 1960s. Being of that age group, I thought it was sensational.

One of the most dangerous experiences I had as a News Bureau photographer came in 1995. I was to photograph the construction of the Stratosphere. At that time, we referred to it as Bob Stupak's Tower. It was no longer Vegas World, but nobody knew what the new name would be. Anyway, I went up in a construction elevator. That in itself was quite an experience. When I reached the top, I realized that the pod was just a couple of cement platforms. I started taking pictures of the construction. Then, I wanted to get a few shots of the Strip. It was windy, so I had to crawl toward the ledge. There was nothing to hold me on the structure. I lost a couple of rolls of film in the wind, but that's all. It was a great view, but I was glad to leave. I've been to a lot of construction sites where I've had to use a hard hat. That particular day, a plastic helmet wouldn't have done me any good if I had fallen.

One night, I was shooting a very lavish party at the Desert Inn. It was a celebration of the hotel's 50th anniversary. A lot of invited guests from the old days of Las Vegas were there. I was busy taking pictures of everyone, including Toni Clark, wife of the original owner Wilbur Clark. She wanted me to take group shots with her friends. The legendary entertainer Keely Smith squeezed into the picture. That was okay with me. She had always been one of my favorites. Keely was a sensational singer, the kind that you never get tired of listening to. She used to live in a very large house on the Desert Inn golf course. Everyone knew which one was hers. It had an oriental look. Anyway, I told her that I often thought about that house. She told me that she did too. Keely and Louis Prima were the most vibrant act that ever played the Sahara's Casbar Lounge. They were the undisputed king and queen of Las Vegas. I was too young to see them live, but I've seen the tapes. A short time after the Desert Inn's birthday party, Keely recorded an album called "Keely Sings Sinatra." I think it received a Grammy Award and was nominated for album of the year. A few years later, I caught up with Frank Sinatra Jr. at the ribbon cutting of Frank Sinatra Drive. After the event, we went to the Bootlegger to have lunch. At the restaurant, Frank Jr. and Lorraine Hunt were interviewed on a local radio show. After the session, I gave him a picture of the Desert Inn marquee the night Frank Sinatra passed away. He appreciated the effort and told me to call him Frank, not Mr. Sinatra. He was very low-key and down to earth. I've crossed paths with a lot of the Sinatra's. I met Nancy, Tina, Frank Jr., and Barbara. I also photographed Frank Sr. That's pretty special for a kid who grew up in Twin Lakes.

In 1993 I was at an art gallery in Caesars Forum and photographed Anthony Quinn. He was showing his personal works of art. While there, I asked him about "Zorba the Greek," the 1964 movie that put him on the map. He told me that everyone thought he was Greek because of his character in the movie. He said that he was actually a Mexican. He chuckled when he told the story. His art was good, but not many celebrities are great artists. Tony Bennett is an exception. Most of them are just selling their name. Another celebrity turned artist was Phyllis Diller. I photographed her at the MGM's art gallery. She was a really nice lady and a Las Vegas veteran entertainer, but her work was not very good. Peter Max, a well-known artist from New York, opened his own gallery in the Forum in 2005. His work is extremely vivid and modern. I photographed him and found him to be very cooperative. He gave me several different poses in front of one of his paintings. "Obviously, he's done this before," I thought. When we finished shooting, he asked me if I was hungry. I said yes, so we found a deli across from his gallery. Peter said that he was a vegetarian, and the chef made him some kind of stew. I ordered what Peter had, and it was actually quite good. We talked for about an hour. He told me all about his gallery in New York. It sounded like a big production. All in all, it was an interesting lunch.

In 1996, I photographed Madonna during the Billboard Awards at the MGM. The credentialed press photographers were only allowed to shoot the red carpet arrivals. But for some unknown reason, I was taken inside to photograph the show itself. It was an obvious mistake, but I didn't say anything. Madonna was actually a surprise guest at the show. That night, she was wearing a one-of-a-kind gown from Italy. I took pictures of her, along with all the other performers and presenters. The next day, someone representing the designer called me at work. Somehow they found out that I was the photographer who was allowed inside, and they offered me $5,000 dollars for the negatives.

Because I was an employee of the News Bureau, I did not take the money. Once in a while, situations like that pop up in a photographer's career. I'm the kind of person that prefers a steady paycheck.

One of my most dramatic photo opportunities happened in December of 1996. The musical "CATS" appeared at the Aladdin Theater for the Performing Arts. The play was a photographer's dream. The set and costumes were so colorful that each photo told its own story. Of the many frames I shot, one stood out from the rest. It was a passionate scene that became timeless. One of the cats suddenly posed and looked at the camera. I got the shot, and that was a career moment for me.

In October of 2000, the El Rancho hotel was imploded. As I watched it go down, I thought about the original El Rancho, which opened in 1941 on the property located across the street from the Sahara. It was called the El Rancho

Vegas and was a single-story hotel on a large piece of land. It was the first resort hotel on the Strip and looked more like a ranch than a hotel. It had major Hollywood stars in its showroom and maintained a luxury yacht on Lake Mead. A fire destroyed the hotel one night in 1960. I remember seeing the ashes the next morning. It was shocking. The lot sat vacant for many years afterward. I never could think of the hotel that was demolished in the year 2000 as the El Rancho. It was a real slum, cheaply built and never maintained. Originally, the Thunderbird hotel was built on that property in 1948. It had entertainers like Rosemary Clooney and Judy Garland in the showroom and a great restaurant called Big Joe's Oyster Bar. The locals liked to hang out at the Thunderbird. They felt comfortable there, which is rare for a hotel on the Strip. In 1977 it became the Silverbird, and the deterioration began. In the end, I didn't understand how a nice hotel like the Thunderbird could end up in shambles and be called the El Rancho. On the same note, the Showboat hotel, located on Boulder Highway, became the Castaways hotel before it was imploded. The original Castaways hotel was a property on the Las Vegas Strip, not on the Boulder Highway. The Showboat is the place where Johnny and I would go bowling when we were kids. It had a huge bowling alley with a lot of lanes. It was very popular with the locals.

One day Manny Cortez, then President of the Las Vegas Convention Center, called me up to his office. He said Nick

Pileggi, author of the movie "Casino," was in town. Manny asked me to go to the Sands hotel and meet Nick at the swimming pool. I got in my car and drove down the Strip. When I arrived at the Sands, I spotted him right away. Nick asked me to take some pictures around the hotel just in case he decided to make another "Casino" type movie. He knew that the hotel was scheduled for implosion in the near future, and he wanted to remember what it looked like. We walked around the property, taking pictures. I included him in some of the shots. When I finally saw the movie "Casino," I wondered how a nice guy like Nick could write such a violent movie. I thought it portrayed a very brutal side of Las Vegas' history. All in all, it was another interesting day at work.

September 30, 2004, started out like any other day. I got up early. I was actually too tired to go to work, but I went anyway. When I arrived, my fellow employees were gathered in the office and snickering among themselves. It wasn't my birthday, but I had a feeling that they were going to pull something on me. The News Bureau received word that actress Elizabeth Hurley was going to be in town to promote Estee Lauder products at the Forum Shops and the Fashion Show Mall. They knew that I had been talking about her for years, and I wanted to meet her. They all came into my office and told me that I was assigned to her all day. I couldn't believe it. It was going to be another good day. I soon packed up my camera gear and went to Neiman Marcus, located in the Fashion Show Mall. At the designated time, Elizabeth Hurley made her entrance. She was a real beauty. She sat down and started signing autographs for those who purchased Estee Lauder products. I didn't get any great photos because I was not able to get in the right position. It was too crowded. After an hour, she left the store and proceeded to the Forum. Once there, she sat at a table inside the Estee Lauder store and signed more autographs. It was a small area, but somehow things worked out for me. I was able to get very close to her and shot some great pictures. I never did talk to her; she seemed too busy. I soon returned to the News Bureau and told everyone the story. I was positive that my Elizabeth Hurley shoot was better than anything they did that day.

In 2004, President Bush made a speech during the National Guard Convention in Las Vegas. Because the event was at the convention center, I was able to photograph him. I had to go through the usual Secret Service credentialing ordeal. They want to know your Social Security number, your date of birth, and a few other things. They check your camera bag and all of its contents. They even take the lenses off the camera bodies and inspect them. Most of the time, you have to leave the area and let the dogs sniff everything. Then, you are allowed back in the room to await the

President. I have gone through it many times; I've photographed a few Presidents.

The year 2009 was the 50th anniversary of the Las Vegas Convention Center. Several employees were selected to place items into a time capsule during the April 14 Board of Directors meeting. I had the honor of representing the Public Affairs Department. I placed an old Rolleiflex camera and a roll of black & white film into the capsule, which would be opened in another 50 years. I felt that it represented the camera most used by News Bureau photographers. I also put a real silver dollar in the capsule. It was significant because silver dollars were so plentiful when I grew up here.

Three weeks before Elton John ended his long-running engagement at the Colosseum showroom in Caesars Palace, I received a call from someone in the executive office. The hotel wanted to give Elton a going-away gift. He collected old black & white photos, so it was only natural for Caesars to think of archival Las Vegas images. They asked my opinion regarding which pictures would be best for the gift, and I sent them some examples to choose from. They ended up picking two images, one of the famous "Welcome to Fabulous Las Vegas" sign taken in 1960 and another of the Caesars Palace marquee in 1966. Victor Borge's name was on that marquee. I had a feeling they would pick that one because Mr. Borge was also a piano player. We quickly printed the pictures. Caesars had them framed and presented the photos to Elton after his last show. They ultimately invited me to attend one of his shows. Debbie and I accepted the invitation and went to a performance the day before he closed. He was very good, especially in that large showroom.

In 2009, I was asked to take some new photos of the Trump Tower. They needed a few room interiors and swimming pool shots. I agreed and did the job. In return, I received a complimentary room and dinner in their restaurant. The room had a great view, so Debbie and I watched the lights on the other hotels that evening. I noticed Ray Romano's name on a marquee and started thinking about the new Las Vegas headliners. I wondered if they were different than the old-timers. In those days, showroom stars performed two shows a night, two weeks at a time. Because they appeared many times a year, they had a chance to develop relationships with hotel employees. The ones that had compassion for the working class gave some type of gift to the employees on closing night. People like Jerry Lewis, Don Rickles, Nancy Sinatra, Charo, and Joey Heatherton always remembered the employees who helped them. I wonder if these new stars care as much about the hotel employees.

March 15 was a Tuesday morning, and I was about to shoot the implosion of the Stardust hotel. It was one of those situations where I didn't have to work that night, but I wanted to. I felt obligated. After all, it was the Stardust. As with the passing of Frank Sinatra, I went to the Strip on my own to photograph a bit of history. At about midnight, I drove to the roof of the parking garage at the Wynn hotel. There were already a lot of people there, but I had called ahead, and members of the Wynn Security Department helped me get situated. As I looked down at the street, it looked like a mob scene because there were so many bodies. I was glad to be on the roof, away from all the turmoil. Right before 2:30 a.m., the fireworks began, and then the countdown started. The fireworks were spectacular, and the countdown was lit on the side of the building. At 2:30 a.m., the Stardust hotel was imploded. Six seconds later, it was gone. Being an implosion veteran, I knew what to do. Immediately, I put my camera equipment in the car and jumped in. Then the implosion dust hit. It was like a sandstorm. The people in the street ran for cover, but the dusty fog rolled over everything in its path. I sat happily in my car until the dust cleared. I knew the Strip would be closed for the next few hours, so I went into the Wynn coffee shop for breakfast. I ordered bacon, eggs, and those great hash brown potatoes that all the hotels served. At about 5:00 a.m., I walked back to my car. The path was clear, so I went back to the News Bureau and sent a couple of shots to AP. They were immediately picked up and ran all around the world. It was a good night because I was shooting something important. I've always thought of myself as a true shooter. I'm not a desk person, and I don't like paperwork. I would rather work all night than sit at a desk. Of my favorite implosions, the Stardust hotel was number four. The Landmark was first. The Dunes Hotel was second, and the Aladdin was third. I love documenting the history of Las Vegas. When historical events happen, I like to be there.

While at the News Bureau, I covered the opening of "The Glass Bridge at Grand Canyon West." It's a curved bridge with a glass-bottom walkway that projects 70 feet out over a section of the Grand Canyon. It is 4,000 feet above the canyon floor and has a spectacular view. For me, it was a long, rugged, and windy day. I departed Las Vegas early and drove two hours to the Hualapai Indian reservation in Arizona. Most of the drive was on a dirt road. Fortunately, I was not in my own car. Once there, I was transported by bus to the Skywalk. Soon afterward, there was a brief and colorful opening ceremony. Astronaut Buzz Aldrin took the first walk on the glass bridge. I quickly followed him. While on the bridge, I was told to wear lightweight booties over my shoes. They were designed to protect the glass from scratches. I also had to keep moving because of the large number of visitors. During my walk, I managed to get some great shots of the bridge and the people on it. After a buffet lunch, I made the exhausting trip back to Las Vegas. When I entered the office, people asked me if I was afraid while on the bridge. I told them that I had been in so many bad situations during my career I no longer feared anything. Then, I quickly sent some pictures to the wire services, where they were picked up immediately. They weren't the best photos I'd ever taken, but they received a lot of international attention. I don't know how AP rates images, but the ones I sent were rated very high. In fact, they were rated higher than any images I ever sent. I must admit, they were pretty dramatic. I guess the trip was worthwhile, after all.

I photographed Judy Collins at the Las Vegas Hilton in 1996. I remember shooting her from the balcony. It was one of the few hotels in those days that had a balcony. I used a long lens, so it didn't matter where I shot from. I photographed her again years later during a Christmas concert at UNLV. After the show, I took some pictures of her with Heather. Judy is famous for her Christmas concerts. It's her favorite time of the year. She enjoyed my dedication, and I enjoyed her taking time for Heather. Where else could things like that happen? Las Vegas has always been a great place for photographers.

The chorus line at the Sands was called the Copa Girls. In 1991, I was sent to the hotel to photograph the girls on stage during the day. They were rehearsing a new routine, and the hotel wanted some pictures. I only had black-and-white film, which worked out to my advantage. Each of the girls had one white stocking, and the other leg was bare. I asked them to get on the stage and pose for me. They lined up and turned sideways. Because of the black-and-white film, and the black-and-white costumes, the picture came out great. It wouldn't have been the same in color. The event was symbolic. It was the last time the News Bureau photographed the famous Sands Copa Girls.

Because I worked the swing shift my first few years at the News Bureau, I photographed most of the shows that came to town. Some of them were more memorable than others. In 1991, I photographed something very special. It happened at the Desert Inn. Fats Domino appeared in the showroom, and the hotel was going to have a surprise birthday celebration for him. Chubby Checker was to bring the cake to him halfway through the show. That night, I arrived at the D.I. and met the publicity director near the entrance of the showroom. He escorted me to the stage, where I crouched down and put my elbows on the stage floor. I was ready to shoot. Soon, Chubby Checker came out from behind the curtains singing and holding a birthday cake. The audience joined the songfest, and I began shooting. Fats turned around from his piano seat to see what was going on. He blew out the candles and thanked Chubby. As I continued to shoot, I couldn't help but notice how nicely they were both dressed. Fats Domino was decked out in a white suit, and Chubby Checker was wearing Levis with a pair of snakeskin boots. When the assignment was over, I went back to the office and developed the film. Years later, I was assigned to photograph Chubby Checker on Fremont Street. Before the show, I talked to him on his bus. I mentioned the Fats Domino event at the Desert Inn, and he remembered it well. They were both very good performers, perfect for Las Vegas.

In 1993, I photographed the Jerry Lewis Labor Day Telethon in the Space Center of the Sahara hotel. Near the end of the show, Steve Lawrence and Eydie Gorme appeared on stage with Jerry Lewis. All three were singing, but Jerry was making funny faces. They were very close together, with Jerry in the middle. I was kneeling on the floor about six feet from them and was trying to stay out of the way of the TV cameras. It was on national television, and I did not want to be in the shots. I took a lot of pictures, but one, in particular, was perfect. All three entertainers had great expressions on their faces. The last time I saw that photo, it was hanging in the hallway near the executive offices of the Las Vegas Convention Center.

I was working at the News Bureau in 1994 when "The Greatest Show on Earth" came to town. I never thought much about the circus until I had a camera in my hand. Then, it became a horse of a different color. On a warm July afternoon, the Ringling Brothers Barnum and Bailey Circus train stopped in the back of Caesars Palace. They needed to get the elephants to the Thomas and Mack Center at UNLV, where they would perform, so they decided to march them down the Strip. I got the photo assignment and drove to the Barbary Coast, where I parked my car and walked out to the street. A few minutes later, the circus performers appeared on the north side of Caesars. They were followed by a long line of elephants. The colorful band of gypsies made their way to the front of the property and turned south on Las Vegas Boulevard. They didn't seem to mind if photographers joined the parade, so I started walking alongside them. I tried to maneuver my way in and out of the elephants, but I couldn't. Each elephant's trunk was wrapped around the tail of the elephant in front of them, making it impossible to get between the large animals. I photographed them for a while and then retreated to my car. It was a very short but exhilarating photo shoot. Seeing elephants walking down the Strip was quite a sight. To me, it felt like a local event because Ringling Brothers Circus was owned by Kenneth Feld. He was Siegfried and Roy's producer, and I had taken many pictures of him in the past.

During the summer of 1994, I traveled to Chicago on business for the Las Vegas Convention Center. I took a lot of photos during the sales events but managed to find some time for myself. Since it was my first trip to the windy city, I tried to see as much of it as I could. I rode a double-decker tour bus and went to the Navy Pier. I also walked through Grant Park and saw Buckingham Fountain. One night, I set up my tri-pod near the Chicago River. The tour boats were parked, and some of the windows in the office buildings were still lit. I wanted to show more drama than beauty, so I used black-and-white film. The pictures came out very well. In fact, I framed one of them and placed it on a wall in my living room. On that trip, I discovered how friendly and accommodating the people of Chicago were. I enjoyed the neighborhoods, the food, and the cultures. I returned to the city many times after that. It's a great place.

Many years after I first saw Bill Cosby, he appeared at the Las Vegas Hilton. The News Bureau needed some current shots, so I went to the showroom and photographed him on stage. He was just as funny as ever. In those days, we were using black and white film. The pictures were very dramatic because there were no distractions. They just showed a simple stage and a man sitting in a chair with funny expressions on his face.

My friend, Lee Ferrell, was a member of the Righteous Brothers band for about forty years. When the group was in town, Lee and I would visit. Most of the time, it was backstage, at a restaurant, or at the News Bureau. He loved all the autographed pictures that were hanging on the walls in the office. Being an entertainer, he appreciated the history of Las Vegas. One day, he told me that his son was in town and asked if he could bring him to the News Bureau to see the collection. Lee told me his son's name was Will, and he was an actor on "Saturday Night Live." I told Heather that Will Ferrell was going to arrive at the News Bureau on a certain day and asked if she would like to meet him. She said yes, and we made plans. When the day arrived, Lee and Will walked from the Hilton to our office at the convention center. Heather was already at the News Bureau waiting. As soon as they came in, Will started looking at all the pictures. There were about a hundred autographed photos, and he stopped and looked at every one of them. I was surprised that he recognized most of the celebrities. After all, they were before his time. It didn't take long before we started joking around. I told him that my favorite sketch on "Saturday Night Live" was a scene from the Winter Olympics in Utah. While skiing in a downhill event, Will was talking to his fellow competitor about the Book of Mormon. It was really funny. Soon, he sat at my desk, and I took a picture of Heather leaning over his shoulder. Then, everybody got into the spirit. Heather sat in the chair, and I handed Lee and Will each a camera. I became the director, and they were the photographers. During the action, we all started laughing. After that, they went back to the hotel. It's a story Heather will never forget.

In 1995 I was on assignment to photograph Muhammad Ali at the Planet Hollywood restaurant in Caesars Forum. He was going to receive a gift, a bronze bust of himself in a boxing pose. The figure was about two feet tall and looked heavy. There were five other photographers there, so it was slightly crowded. We waited for about half an hour, and then Ali walked in. He was wearing a dark suit and sunglasses. He didn't say anything but posed long enough for all the photographers to get their shots. I used black and white film and took some classic photos of him holding the bronze statue. I couldn't miss it; he was only standing five feet in front of me. He had a great smile.

As far as golf photography, I've done a lot. I have taken pictures of the PGA, LPGA, and SENIOR Tours. My list is too numerous to name, but I photographed most of the professionals of my era. I would love to have been a photographer in the 1920s when Bobby Jones was playing. He was a very special person. My favorite players to photograph on the PGA tour were Fred Couples, Payne Stewart, and John Daly. The LPGA favorites were Annika Sorenstam, Natalie Gulbis and Julie Inkster. The SENIOR tour included Arnold Palmer, Jack Nicklaus, and Chi-Chi Rodriguez. My favorite golf shot was of Payne Stewart lining up a putt, looking directly at me. I positioned myself across the green from him; therefore, it looked as if the ball was coming right at the camera. He dressed like an old-time golfer, which made the photo even more interesting.

I worked at the Davis Cup Tennis Tournament event at Caesars Palace in 1995. I photographed a few matches and got everything I was supposed to. The tight shots were finished, but I wanted to show the stadium with Caesar's hotel tower in the background. The tennis court was so big that I needed a fisheye lens. It worked out perfectly, and I got a historical picture with a Hasselblad camera. After all, the Davis Cup is a rare event in Las Vegas. Years later, Las Vegas sponsored a float in the Rose Parade. I got the assignment, and Debbie and I went to Pasadena. On New Year's morning, Debbie sat in the stands, but I was standing in a designated spot on the street with the other photographers. As our float passed by, I used the same fisheye lens as the Davis Cup. Our float was enormous, and I was standing right next to it. As usual, I got lucky, and everything worked out fine.

The longest News Bureau assignment I ever had lasted an entire week. In 1996 the Miss Universe Pageant was in town, and there were numerous events attached to it. Besides the shoots all around the city, there was a group shot at the Rio hotel swimming pool. Before the girls took their positions on the bleachers, they were milling around the pool area. I saw three of them huddled together, so I asked if I could take a picture with them. I handed my camera to another photographer, and he took the photo. In the shot, I was surrounded by Miss Sweden, Miss Cayman Islands, and Miss Bahamas. I was wearing my SAE shirt that day, so I sent the photo to the national office. It was published in the fraternity magazine, and I received a lot of phone calls from around the country. I guess the picture was a big hit.

My favorite rock & roll photo was taken in 1997. The Rolling Stones were scheduled to perform at the MGM, and I received media credentials. I was thrilled because they were one of my favorite groups. They were in the middle of their "Bridges to Babylon" tour, and I couldn't wait to photograph them. It's more difficult to photograph a group of entertainers than a single person. Getting them all in one shot is easy, but capturing the right moment is a challenge. Each member of a band should look good. In reality, someone usually has their eyes closed or a look on their face that is not flattering. On the night of November 22, 1997, I was escorted into the arena with other photographers. We were placed in front of the stage and tried not to disturb the audience. We were only allowed to shoot the first three songs; we all knew the routine. When the Rolling Stones came out, I had to concentrate. I forced myself to block out the excitement of the moment and get some newsworthy photos.

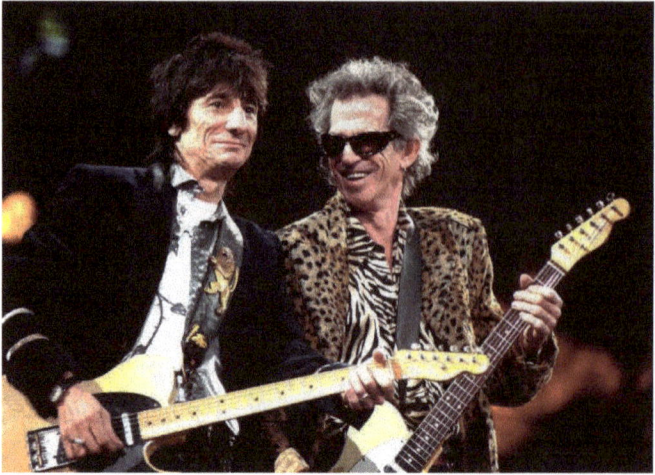

Of the many colorful photos I shot, one, in particular, told the story. Keith Richards and Ronnie Wood came together for a split second. They both had great smiles, and the lighting was perfect. I immediately knew that I had gotten the shot. I already captured quality images of Mick Jagger and Charlie Watts, so the event was a success. As usual, I sent the photos to the wires. That night was one of my personal favorite assignments. I was so excited that I couldn't sleep. A few days later, I sent the photos to their London office and received a nice letter of gratitude.

In 1998 I took four showgirls to the "Welcome to Fabulous Las Vegas" sign. I posed them in front of it and took some pictures. I think the News Bureau paid them each six hundred dollars for three hours. After shooting at the sign, we found a spot in front of the Luxor and took more photos. The pictures came out great. It was the beginning of several opportunities to photograph showgirls at the

Welcome sign. There's something about showgirls and the Welcome sign that go together like bacon and eggs.

It was May 14, 1998. The morning news spread across Las Vegas like wildfire; Frank Sinatra had just died. Because he had been sick for such a long time, the hotels already had the plan to eulogize him. Through their collected efforts spearheaded by the News Bureau, the hotels would dim their exterior lights for a one-minute tribute to the man who helped turn this small desert town into the "Entertainment Capital of the World." By early afternoon, most of the marquees were glowing with his image, and larger-than-normal crowds gathered on Las Vegas Boulevard. I had already worked a full day, but I felt a need to document this moment in history. After all, it was my town also. I put my camera equipment in the car and drove to the Strip. I parked at the Flamingo and walked across the street to Caesars Palace. I set my camera on a tripod and waited with other members of the media. At 8:30 p.m., the testimonial began. One by one, the hotel lights dimmed. Caesars Palace, Harrah's, The Mirage, The Imperial Palace, and The Flamingo were suddenly dark. The tourists driving down the street began honking their horns to add their personal touch to the event. It was quite a scene. Las Vegas had suddenly taken on a spiritual essence.

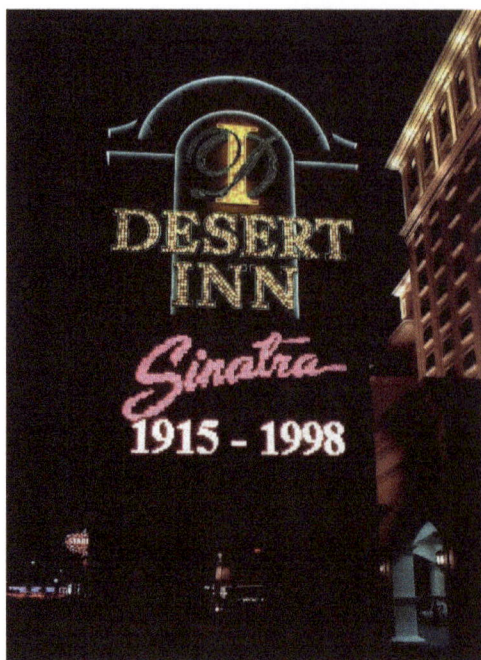

While watching the event unfold, I remember the time I was in the same room with Frank Sinatra. Nancy appeared at the Sahara, and he wanted to see her perform. That particular night, word came down that Mr. Sinatra would be in the audience but did not want to be recognized. The plan was for him to enter the showroom after the house lights went out. He would watch the show, and then he would leave before the final number. Nobody would realize that he was in the showroom. At midnight, the lights went dark, and the show started. Frank and his party quietly entered the room and were escorted to their booth. For some reason, the Maitre d' thought Frank needed special treatment, so he pulled the waiter from his station and replaced him with a Captain who hadn't served a drink in fifteen years. That's when the problems began. Soon the Captain appeared. He took their order and went into the kitchen. A short time later, he returned with some drinks and a bottle of wine. He served the drinks but struggled with the wine and spilled it on Frank. Another Captain came to the rescue, but it was too late. The damage had already been done. Frank looked at them and said, "Leave me alone. I just came to see the show." With that, the Captains apologized and left the room. As I watched the melee, I couldn't help but think that the waiter should have been left at his station, and everyone would have been happy, especially Mr. Sinatra. When the show ended, Frank was gone, and the employees were the only ones who knew what had happened. It didn't seem important at the time, but for me, it became one of those situations that I'll never forget. Back on the Strip, it was suddenly 8:31 p.m., and the tribute to Frank was finished. The hotel lights came on, and the traffic began to flow in its usual manner. After a short conversation with another photographer, I walked back to the Flamingo and put my camera equipment in the car. I then drove past the hotels one last time to absorb the significance of the event. As I passed the Desert Inn, I took a photo of their marquee. It ended up being one of my personal favorites of all time.

In 1999, Shania Twain appeared at the MGM Grand. She was young, and I didn't know who she was. For her concert, I didn't need a long lens. The press photographers were escorted to a section in front of the first row of seats. When she appeared, I was resting my elbows on the stage. As she started singing, I realized that I was a bit too close. During one song, she came to my side of the stage. I had to move my hand, or she would have stepped on it. She reminded me of Mick Jagger. They both move around quite a bit during their performances. Sometimes it's hard to hit a moving target. After that night, I knew who she was.

In 1999, I photographed Tommy Tune at the MGM. He was starring in a show called EFX. He was a Broadway star, so I didn't know much about him. I didn't realize how tall he was. I quickly found out that he was six feet, six inches tall. For a dancer, that's all legs. I was using a 400 mm lens from the back of the room. For one moment during the show, he looked right at the camera. I snapped the picture, and it became a classic. It was just one of those shots that worked. Everything fit together for an instant. He was dressed in white with a yellow background. It was a vertical shot, which made him look even taller. When people see the picture, they don't realize how far I was from the stage. I saw him at an event a short time later, and he signed the picture to the News Bureau.

It was only one day until News Year's Eve, and I didn't know where I was going to be when the century turned. The News Bureau photographers had a lot of good ideas, but we decided not to finalize the assignments until we were sure that our photos would show the best pictorial coverage of the event. Then fate dealt its hand. The Paris Las Vegas hotel announced that confetti would fall from the Eiffel Tower at the stroke of midnight. Suddenly, the intersection of Las Vegas Boulevard and Flamingo Road became the center of the universe. This was before fireworks were launched on the Strip. The photo assignments were then handed out, and I got the job. A few minutes later, I drove to Bally's hotel to scout out the shot. Their public relations manager met me at the bell desk and escorted me to the roof. As soon as I saw the view, I realized that I had the opportunity to document a very special moment in history. I thanked the publicist and returned to the News Bureau to prepare for my assignment. The next day, I arrived at Bally's in the early afternoon. I found a parking spot and proceeded to the roof, where I unpacked my camera equipment. It was already cold outside, so I decided to spend the next few hours in the hotel room that Bally's provided for members of the media. At about five o'clock, the sun began to set, so I went back on the roof and started shooting pictures of the city lights. At the time, there was nothing else to do. The next several hours, I spent alternating my time between the chilly rooftop and the warmth of the hotel room. Eventually, I was joined by members of the Fox network. We shared coffee and sandwiches provided by the Room Service department. At 11:45 p.m., I walked to the roof for the final time. I loaded my camera with film, attached a wide-angle lens, and looked through the viewfinder. What I saw was overwhelming. The passion for the event and the beauty of the city suddenly came to life. I knew I was in the right place at the right time. The Strip was now full of people. The Bellagio fountains began a dazzling water show, and the clock on their marquee began counting down. I held my cable release and waited. At midnight the crowds cheered to a deafening pitch. The Bellagio clock turned to the year 2000, and confetti poured out of the Eiffel Tower. It was a sight to behold. The confetti was lit up like fireworks from the lights below. I began shooting picture after picture and managed to get off three rolls of film. At that time, we still used film cameras. A few minutes later, it was all over. The confetti disappeared, and the crowds moved on. I packed up my equipment, took one last look at the city, and quietly walked away, knowing I got the shot of the century.

In December of 2003, it snowed in Las Vegas. It seemed like a good photo opportunity, so I drove to the Bali Hai golf course on the south end of the Strip. I wanted to show the rest of the country a very unusual image of Las Vegas, and I thought a golf course covered in snow was the best shot. As I drove to the course, the snow started to melt. I didn't know if I would make it or not. Some of the snow on Las Vegas Boulevard was already gone. Fortunately, it stuck to the grass, and the fairways were still white. In the pro shop, I introduced myself and asked if I could use one of their golf carts. They gave me a cart, and I drove out to one of the holes. I looked back at the city and knew I was in the right place. In the picture, the flag stick was in the foreground, and Mandalay Bay was in the background. Everything else was white. It was exactly the shot I wanted. I quickly took some pictures and went back to the office. I sent the best one to AP. A couple of hours later, the snow disappeared. Some situations are like that. You have to take advantage of them while you can. A few years later, it snowed again. This time I went to the "Welcome to Fabulous Las Vegas" sign and captured a very unusual photo. It's not often that the famous sign is surrounded by snow.

Celine Dion opened the Caesars Palace Colosseum in 2003. I took pictures of her at a press conference afterward and sent the pictures to AP. I worked with her a couple of times before that. The first time, Caesars wanted me to take photos of her in her dressing room. Normally that was an easy request, but that particular day I was in New York. They called the house, and Heather told them that I would do it. I think she just wanted to meet Celine. Anyway, I arrived home that evening and was told to go to Caesars as soon as my plane landed. Heather and I marched into her dressing room, ready for action. I photographed her holding a deck of cards for some kind of publicity shot. It must have been something very casual because she was in her bathrobe. While we were with her, she autographed a CD for Heather. The night was a success. After that, we went home, and New

York City was just a distant memory. The year before the Colosseum opened, I took pictures of Celine wearing a hard hat and holding a jackhammer. Caesars was publicizing the construction of the Colosseum, and members of the press were invited. She seemed to know how to handle the jackhammer. It looked pretty heavy to me. After the shoot, we all had lunch. Celine Dion has always been great to work with.

I enjoyed construction photography. It made me feel that I was getting a glimpse of the future. I also realized that many years from the construction date, someone would want to see the photos. The pictures are actually important documents. They cannot be re-shot. I photographed different stages of the Luxor during its construction. It was one of the most interesting hotels to shoot because of the pyramid and the sphinx. The images of Paris Las Vegas were memorable because of the Eiffel Tower, and New York-New York had its own version of the Statue of Liberty. I was lucky to have seen these properties being built. I've also taken photos of Excalibur, MGM Grand, Bellagio, Monte Carlo, Wynn, Encore, Palazzo, and Venetian while they were under construction. Each one took on its own character as it slowly came to life.

I've photographed Engelbert Humperdinck twice. The first time was at Bally's hotel. After the show, I went to his dressing room and took pictures of him playing darts with some people from England. He was a real gentleman, and it was an easy shoot. The second time I photographed Engelbert was a little more interesting. I received a call from someone on his staff. It really took me by surprise. I felt like Al Stump when Ty Cobb called and wanted him to write his biography. This time, they wanted me to photograph Engelbert's show at the Orleans. It was his 70th birthday, and they wanted pictures of the event. To this day, I don't know how they got my name and phone number; maybe they remembered me from previous years. I told them that I was retired from freelance work, and I recommended other photographers. It seems they wouldn't take no for an answer. They called again. This time I gave in and shot the show. As usual, I ended up in his dressing room. His family was there, and I took some birthday pictures. That night, Engelbert and I talked about the dart board photos at Bally's and how long ago it seemed. The next day, I gave him a disc filled with photos. I was paid cash for the job, and that seemed like the end of it. About three months later, I received a call from another member of his staff. She asked if I would allow them to use the pictures from the Orleans. It didn't matter to me, so I said yes. After all, I was retired from that kind of stuff. I never did find out what they used them for. He was a joy to work with.

It was business as usual at work. I had been rummaging through the pictorial history of Las Vegas and printing the best photographs for some future displays. My endeavor started weeks earlier. Up to that point, I had printed about 700 of the 1,000,000 archival negatives the News Bureau possessed. Suddenly, I came across a photo that brought the entire project to a halt. All the elements that make a perfect photograph were right in front of me. The composition, the lighting, the quality of the negative, the pose, and the subject all came together in one breathtaking image. It was a blonde woman dressed in a white evening gown, holding a giant base fiddle against a black background. I couldn't believe it; I had just found the most beautiful photo in the history of Las Vegas. I immediately made a print and showed it to the office staff. They agreed that the picture was indeed special, but nobody knew who the mystery woman was.

After some research, we discovered that the photo was taken at the Rivera hotel in 1957, and the blonde bombshell was Mamie Van Doren. Most people would have left it at that, but I wanted to know more. "Where is she now?" I thought. "Would she like to see the photo? Would she be willing to autograph it?" I had to find out. As fate would have it, I had a meeting scheduled with Rat Pack member Joey Bishop later in the week to help me identify people in the archival photos. I needed to talk to him anyway, so I picked up the phone and called him. I asked Joey if he knew the whereabouts of Mamie. If so, what were the chances of meeting her? Much to my delight, Joey said that she lived near him and he would ask her to come to his house on the day of our get-together. A few days later, I traveled to Joey's house in Newport Beach, armed with hundreds of vintage Las Vegas photographs. When I arrived, he invited me in, and we quickly went to work. Not more than five minutes passed when the doorbell rang. Joey walked to the door, opened it, and said, "Hi, Mamie." I couldn't believe my eyes; there stood the woman in the picture. She introduced herself to me, and then we all sat on the floor in the living room. I watched as Joey and Mamie identified more people than I thought possible. Joey was witty and had a funny story for each situation. Mamie was as friendly and beautiful as I hoped she would be. That day Mamie and I became instant friends. We exchanged phone numbers and promised future meetings. It was truly incredible; a million-to-one chance worked out. I beat the odds. I found Mamie Van Doren.

The day after Mamie helped us identify people in the Las Vegas photos, Joey and I had the house to ourselves. Sylvia went shopping, so we sat down and watched some tapes from "The Joey Bishop Show." It was a television comedy from 1961 to 1965. I enjoyed the show when I was young, and it was very special to have Joey comment on it while we watched it. Eventually, he took me upstairs to see his Rat Pack room. It contained a lot of memorabilia, including awards, photos, and golf trophies. He belonged to the

Newport Beach Country Club and loved golf. As for the photos, there were more Rat Pack images than I had ever seen. He was a member of the group and was very proud of his relationship with Frank Sinatra. He then showed me where he was going to put the new Rat Pack pictures I had given him. It was Joey's special room, and I was thrilled to be invited to see it. Soon it was lunchtime, so we went to the kitchen, where he made ham sandwiches. I knew Joey was Jewish, but I didn't say anything about the ham. We both sat at the kitchen table and began to eat. Suddenly, I sensed that there was something wrong. Joey had a cat. It seemed friendly, but things were just not right. The cat gave me dirty looks. I finally asked Joey what I did to offend the cat. He said that I was sitting in the cat's chair. I immediately moved to another place at the table, and all was well. The cat jumped onto his chair, and we all enjoyed lunch. At his age, Joey was very rigid in his daily routine. He ate lunch at the same time every day and only drank coke from a can. It didn't bother me, although I preferred mine in a glass with ice. One of the pictures I gave him was taken at the Desert Inn golf course a long time ago. It was a photo of him and Harpo Marx clowning around on the driving range. He told me that Harpo was one of his heroes and that they were very good friends. He loved that picture and appreciated my efforts. Joey Bishop was a great host. He was a gentleman and a top-notch comedian. I enjoyed my time with him. It was a privilege to have known him.

During my years as a photographer, I covered a lot of special events in Laughlin. Most of the time, participants would allow members of the press to go for rides during Media Day. I loved the hot air balloon races and took advantage of the invitation each time it was offered. Once, I accepted an invitation to ride in a dune buggy. I had never had an off-road experience and thought it would be exhilarating. I envisioned a scenic ride around the course. I was wrong. It didn't matter that I was a member of the media. That day, I was a co-pilot. I should have realized that it was going to be a rough ride when they strapped me in and gave me a helmet. The only good thing about the entire affair was the fact that the helmet was air-conditioned. The driver took me around the course as fast as the car could go without crashing. The ride rattled my brain and hurt my spine. I was an athletic person, but I was glad when the ride was over. That day, I promised myself that I wouldn't do that again.

While at the News Bureau, I photographed top fuel dragsters at the Las Vegas Motor Speedway. They had seven thousand horsepower and were hitting speeds of 330 miles per hour. The dragsters I saw were notorious for the deafening noise they created. I witnessed it firsthand. They were so powerful that the force actually knocked some of the photographers off their feet. It's hard to describe. Nothing can prepare you for that kind of power. Standing next to the starting line was a dangerous place to be, but that's where the best pictures were. It was the most intense event I had ever photographed, and it all started at Saint Joseph's School with the Soap Box Derby.

In 2006, a week before Cirque du Soleil opened Beatles LOVE at the Mirage, I photographed the pre-show activities. Being a Beatles fan, this was one photo assignment that I didn't want to miss. The musical masterminds of the production were Sir George Martin and his son, Giles Martin. George was the producer of all but one of the Beatles' records, so it was fitting that he was involved in the new show. I really enjoyed meeting him during his press conference. While I was backstage, I photographed all the costumes and props. I also shot the sneak preview, which was only open to members of the media and a few invited guests. I enjoyed the production so much that I saw it four times.

A very strange News Bureau photo assignment occurred with Robert Goulet. He had just completed an evening of Camelot, which I believe was at the Cashman Theater. There was an after-party event at the Excalibur, which was one of the most interesting dinners I've ever seen. They had a lavish banquet that made me feel like I was living in medieval times. Mr. Goulet was at the head table with a menagerie of live birds and large animals. Everyone was dressed in period costumes, but it was the animals that made the dinner so stunning. Usually, animals are not allowed at the dinner table.

When I went to college, I liked the music of a rock group called the Jefferson Airplane. They were a San Francisco band with a stunning lead singer named Grace Slick. In her early life, Grace was an art student. In 1965, she joined a group called The Great Society. Grace provided vocals, played guitar, and wrote a majority of their songs. A year later, she joined the Jefferson Airplane. Grace provided many songs for the group, especially "White Rabbit" and "Some Body to Love." The songs became instant hits, and the rest is history. Years later, the band members went their separate ways, and Grace pursued her art career. Many years after that, I met her at the opening of The Art of Music in the Forum at Caesars Palace. The store sponsored an event to showcase the art of Grace Slick. That night I arrived early, as did Grace. We were introduced, and then we walked into a hallway behind the store. Grace leaned against the wall, lit a cigarette, and starter talking about her art. I suddenly had the queen of rock & roll all to myself. I found her to be a very real and open person. She dressed casually and spoke her mind. I liked her right away. Later in the evening, I positioned her in front of a painting, and we did a mini photo shoot. At the designated time, the doors opened, and the invited guests were allowed in, including Mayor Oscar

Goodman. Eventually, there was a ribbon cutting, and then the reception began. Grace paints with vivid colors. She can paint anything but specializes in rock stars such as Janis Joplin, Jimi Hendrix, and Jim Morrison. Her many portraits of Alice in Wonderland characters are my personal favorites. Before the event was over, she took a picture with me and signed my ticket stub with the inscription "Remember what the dormouse said." The next time I saw Grace was at an art gallery in the Planet Hollywood hotel. We took more pictures and talked about a particular painting of hers called "Golden Gate." I told her that I had purchased it in Hawaii. I picked that piece because the subject is the Golden Gate Bridge in San Francisco. There is also an image of a white rabbit in the lower right corner, just above her signature. She told me that she loves to paint bunnies. Grace is also available for special requests, although they must be very strange in nature. I wanted to talk longer, but she was in town to see the Beatles LOVE show, and her time was short. The last time I saw her was at the Mirage. It was another event to highlight her work. I asked her if she would be willing to paint a white rabbit playing golf. She said that she would be happy to do it. I never actually followed through with it because I knew I couldn't afford it. Some people are beyond words. Grace Slick is one of them.

One of the few times that the hotels interacted with each other was the day of Robert Goulet's funeral. The Public

Relations department of the Las Vegas Convention Center asked for a city-wide tribute. On the designated day, the hotel marquees showed his face and a small quote about Bob for fifteen minutes beginning at noon. I went to the corner of Tropicana and the Strip to capture the moment. Realizing I could only take a few pictures in a short amount of time, I shot the marquees of the MGM Grand and the Excalibur. I then went back to the office and sent the shots to the wire services. AP picked them up right away, and the Review-Journal used one of them on their front page the next morning. I guess their photographers were busy with the funeral itself. As small as it was, I felt good about my part in the entire process. Bob Goulet was a local guy, and I had photographed him many times. He was one of the good guys. I was happy to contribute to his memorial.

On November 13th, 2007, I witnessed another Las Vegas hotel implode into history. This time it was the Frontier. I checked into the office at 11:00 p.m. and collected my equipment. I then drove to a designated site between the Frontier and Trump Tower. Once there, I set my camera on a tripod alongside other members of the media. Someone handed out goggles, hats, and plastic raincoats. At 2:30 a.m., the Frontier was imploded amongst a burst of fireworks. Along with it went some great memories. As usual, I traveled back to the News Bureau and sent the photos out on the wire. Another chapter of my working life was officially closed.

I've always enjoyed personal challenges, little things that most people wouldn't think too much about. Working at the News Bureau put me in a position where I could create such situations. One unlikely event happened on a clear morning in November of 2007. I knew that some people had access to the top of the Luxor hotel. The pyramid-shaped building had a very small area at the top that housed a powerful beam of light. I always wanted to take pictures from that spot. After several emails, I got permission to go there. I met an employee in the hotel lobby and was taken to the guest elevator. We got out on the top floor and went through a locked door. We then began to climb a series of ladders. After a few minutes, we reached the room at the top. It was so small that I couldn't stand up, but the view was everything I had hoped for. One of the window washers opened a window for me, and I took some photos. When I finished, we climbed back down to the top floor. I felt great because the challenge was a success. Once again, I had been in a place that most people would never have access to.

Another great visual assignment happened in 2007. Las Vegas became the only city to host an NBA All-Star Game that was not an NBA franchise city. There was NBA signage all around town, but the biggest and most impressive sight was at New York-New York. They draped the Statue of Liberty with a gigantic NBA All-Star jersey. I checked in at 6:30 a.m., got my camera, and went to the Strip. I stood on the Tropicana property, and I took a picture of the uniform on the Statue of Liberty. I then sent it on the AP wire. It looked great in the Yahoo News section. During NBA All-Star week, the league pulled some good old-fashioned publicity stunts. Reggie Miller, the great basketball star, dressed up like Elvis at the Graceland wedding chapel. He surprised a lucky couple by attending their service. Besides me, the NBA had a video crew there to capture the moment. Seeing Reggie wearing a wig, sunglasses, and a white jumpsuit was very funny. He was laughing up a storm as he tried to fit into something that was made for a shorter person. But the highlight came when he danced down the aisle like Elvis Presley. It was a good stunt because it was fun, and there was no pressure on anybody.

I shot a lot of assignments at hospitals, especially Sunrise. Traditionally, the Las Vegas Bowl teams would go there for community outreach programs. The football players gave away shirts and hats to the children. One of my favorite trips to Sunrise Hospital happened during NBA All-Star week. I had to leave an assignment on a golf course and go to the hospital to photograph the Mayor and several NBA players giving gifts to the children. I decided to follow Mayor Goodman, Scottie Pippen, and Ruth Riley from the WNBA. There were many photographers moving around, but I stuck with my group. We went into most of the rooms on the pediatrics floor, and the celebrities handed out goodies. Someone with the NBA was pulling a little red wagon full of stuffed animals, so I asked Scottie, the Mayor, and Ruth to get down on one knee and pose beside the wagon. They started laughing and tried their best. Scottie said, "After seventeen years, it's kind of hard, but I'll manage." They were all good sports about it. They got down on one knee and posed with the toys. I shot the picture and thought that it was really fun. Another time, I photographed the world's smallest horse at the Sunrise Children's Hospital. The kids loved it, but I thought the horse was a little grumpy. It tried to bite a few times. I think it had an inferiority complex.

On the last night of December 2007, I was at Mix Nightclub on top of the Mandalay Bay Hotel. It was time to photograph the New Year's fireworks, now called "America's Party." Mix was a great place to shoot from because of the spectacular view. As usual, I had to be there a few hours early. Standing outside in the cold wasn't really bad. I had a chance to take some new pictures of the Strip. It was the pounding in my chest from the loud music that was overwhelming. At midnight, the fireworks began. I shot picture after picture and used a four-second exposure to capture the complete span of each burst. When the smoke cleared, I walked to my car and drove back to the News Bureau. I sent my best shot to the wires at about 1:30 a.m. After that, I called it a night and went home. I was tired, cold, and dirty, but it was worth it. The picture came out great. I was very lucky to get into Mix. New Year's parties are usually reserved for paying customers, and press credentials are difficult to come by.

In November of 2009, I was assigned to photograph Iraq war veterans at Wayne Newton's house. Wayne took over where Bob Hope left off. He succeeded Mr. Hope as Chairman of the USO Celebrity Circle. That day, I drove to his house early to make sure I didn't miss anything. I was granted access to his estate and parked by the horse stables. At about noon, the busses arrived filled with soldiers. I began to take pictures, but I saw things that made me feel very humble. A lot of the service people had missing limbs. What I thought was going to be a joyful occasion was suddenly heart-wrenching. They all seemed so young. The troops were treated to sandwiches and soft drinks. They enjoyed the quiet surroundings, but they really loved a little creature that was walking around the grounds. He was Charlie, the penguin. Charlie was both social and lovable. Everyone wanted to touch the little guy. It was nice to see them having a good time. Soon, Wayne made his appearance. He talked to each one of his guests and posed for hundreds of photos. He then brought out one of his Arabian horses. It was easily the most beautiful horse I had ever seen. It pranced around the corral like a superstar. Fortunately, I was one of the lucky people who got up close and personal with the horse. I saw many other horses that day, but the young black beauty was the centerpiece. All in all, everyone was happy to be there. Wayne Newton was a great host.

December of 2009 was very busy at the News Bureau. Even though the National Finals Rodeo was in town, it was the NASCAR Sprint Cup Series Awards and the opening of CityCenter that took the spotlight. I spent many hours documenting the events. I photographed the NASCAR drivers at the Las Vegas Motor Speedway, on the Strip, and at the Wynn hotel. My camera captured so many images of CityCenter that I quit counting. I shot the project from the roofs of Planet Hollywood, the MGM, and the Tropicana. I attended all the press events and shot the interiors of each building. Taking the pictures was easy. Getting the images to the proper media outlets was very time-consuming.

Debbie and I attended the opening night VIP party at Aria hotel in CityCenter. It was a grand event. The restaurants served appetizers, and the bars were open. There were five thousand invitations sent out, and it looked like everyone was there. A few days later, we drove to Newport Beach for a winter getaway. We stayed at Mike's house, even though he wasn't in town. Debbie and Heather had dinner at the Bay Club and watched the Christmas boat parade, but I was a little under the weather. We also walked on the beach and went shopping at the mall. It was good to get away from work for a while.

My assignment for New Year's Eve 2009 was to shoot the fireworks display from the top of the Trump Hotel in Las Vegas. Because of the crowds, I arrived early and sat in the lobby for a couple of hours. A few minutes before midnight, I was escorted to the roof, where I set my camera and tripod on a ledge overlooking the Strip. The fireworks started on time, and I took about twenty pictures. After the first minute of fireworks, there is usually too much smoke in the air to continue shooting. When they finished, I went down to valet parking, got into my car, and drove to the office. I sent a couple of images to AP and then drove home. It was a nice way to end 2009 and begin 2010. I didn't have to mingle with the crowds on the Strip.

February 19th, 2010, was a long but interesting day. I photographed Barack Obama up close and personal for the third time within a couple of years. I took pictures of him at Springs Preserve and Cashman Field as a Presidential candidate, but this was his first time as the President of the United States. All three assignments had a common thread. I was within six feet of him each time. That particular day started out early. I dropped off my camera equipment at about 5:30 a.m. at the ARIA hotel. After that, I was told to leave, so the equipment could be inspected by the Secret Service. At 9:30 a.m., I returned to the area with the rest of the press photographers. We sat there until 11:30 a.m. I was then escorted to a hallway behind the stage, where I waited for another half hour. At noon, the pool photographers who travel with the President joined me. We quickly went into a room where MGM/Mirage employees were already shaking hands with the President. Mr. Obama was moving fast, so I had to take pictures in a hurry. We did the same thing in two other rooms. Finally, we were taken into a large convention room where the President was about to speak. I knelt down in front of the stage and waited for the festivities to begin. There were about forty people seated behind the podium, including Rossi Ralenkotter, Senator Harry Reid, and MGM/Mirage CEO Jim Murren. After speeches by Reid and Murren, the President entered the room. He walked to the podium and began to speak. I took about three hundred pictures of him during his address. I knew there had to be a good Presidential image somewhere in my camera. After the event finished, I went into a small room with three MGM/Mirage employees and downloaded my photos to their computers. They needed the images for their corporate newsletter. I returned to the News Bureau by 2:00 p.m. and downloaded the pictures to my own computer. It was one of those days when everything worked out well. I worked with the Secret Service many times in the past, so I was familiar with the routine. I also took home a great souvenir, a White House press credential.

On March 11th, 2010, Rossi and Mary Jo invited Debbie and me to be their guests at Bishop Gorman's annual Knight of the Gael at the Red Rock Resort. The event is a benefit for Bishop Gorman High School and inducts couples, individuals, and foundations into the Royal Order of the Gael in appreciation for their commitment and dedication to the school. It was a very formal evening, which included a cocktail reception, dinner, and speeches. A lot of people that I knew attended, so I had a chance to engage in some great conversations. We sat with Rossi and Mary Jo and enjoyed the evening very much. The Gorman community honored Frank Fertitta Jr. for his leadership and financial support. I didn't shoot the event for the News Bureau; I just enjoyed myself.

I photographed a professional baseball between the Chicago Cubs and the Chicago White Sox at Cashman Field on March 12th, 2010. It was only a spring training game, but it was still professional baseball. I always felt at home on baseball fields because of my own experience and my love for the game. Therefore, I was very happy with the assignment. I arrived at the stadium at about 5:00 p.m. and picked up my credential. I then walked through the Cubs dugout and onto the field. Once there, I took some pictures of the players warming up and taking batting practice. At 6:00 p.m., I went up to the LVCVA hospitality area and enjoyed a great meal. At about 6:30 p.m., Heather and her friend joined me for some delicious treats before the game. I then made my way back to the field and photographed a cast member from the musical Jersey Boys, who sang the National Anthem. I also shot a comedian named Frank Caliendo as he threw out the symbolic first pitch. At 7:05 p.m., the game started, and I took about eighty pictures of various situations. During the third inning, I walked up to the press box and photographed the convention center's Vice President of Public Affairs, Vince Alberta. He was being interviewed by the Cubs and White Sox radio announcers regarding tourism in Las Vegas. After the interview, I took some pictures of people in the stands. Kids were holding signs in support of their favorite team, so I captured some very cute images. In the bottom of the sixth inning, I returned to the hospitality area and had a little dessert. By then, my assignment was finished, and I had left the ballpark. I got some nice shots and had a good time. All photo assignments should be like that.

August of 2010 was most unusual. I shot some events that were pretty rugged. The Miss Universe Pageant was in town, and I knew that I would be working long hours. To kick things off, I photographed the contestants at the famous "Welcome to Fabulous Las Vegas" sign. Even though it was a morning photo shoot, the air temperature was hot. There were also shadows from the nearby trees covering some of the girls, so the lighting was difficult. All in all, I got lucky and captured some nice images. A few days later, I traveled with the same group to the Valley of Fire. We rode in a caravan of vehicles provided by Pink Jeep Tours. Once there, we made three stops for photo opportunities. The desert temperature was above one hundred degrees, but this time we were in the middle of nowhere. I didn't panic, and neither did the girls. We were in good hands. I took some dramatic shots of the contestants climbing on the giant rock formations and walking in the sand. Somehow, we all survived. The following Monday was the pageant at Mandalay Bay. After waiting for two hours, I was escorted into the Events Center with the other photographers. I shot all of the activities within the event. In the end, a girl from Mexico was crowned as Miss Universe.

In between the Miss Universe photo shoots, I attended media day at the Hoover Dam Bypass Bridge. It was scheduled to open in the near future as the Mike O'Callaghan-Pat Tillman Memorial Bridge, and I was invited to preview the massive project. Being a desert rat, I went there well prepared for the blazing desert sun. I took plenty of water and used a lot of Coppertone. I was given a hard hat and vest as I walked onto the structure. It was an excellent view of the entire area, and I took plenty of pictures of the bridge, the dam, and the surrounding mountains. The moment was historic and well worth the effort.

A couple of weeks before the 2010 MDA Telethon, Candi Cazau called the News Bureau and informed Lisa Jacob that Jerry Lewis wanted to see me. After reviewing my schedule, I decided to visit him on Thursday, August 26th. That afternoon, I arrived at the South Point Hotel and was quickly escorted to the MDA offices in the convention area. I had been in the same situation many times in the past, so it felt like a real Homecoming.

I was greeted by Claudia Stabile, Jerry's long-time Manager, and Jerry Weinberg, President and CEO of the

Muscular Dystrophy Association. We had a nice visit while waiting for Jerry. In a few minutes, he walked into the room. He gave me a big hug, and we talked for a while. Jerry was then interviewed by a writer from the Review Journal. As I watched the interview, I could see some of the personalities that Jerry portrayed in his movies. Herbert Heebert answered questions, as did Gerald Clamson and Captain Eddie. Nobody else was aware of all the great things that were happening. I always loved being around Jerry and his many characters. During the interview, he turned and asked me about Heather. I just happened to have a picture of both of them in his dressing room at the Sahara in 1978. He made sure everyone saw the photo. Even though Jerry Lewis was 84 years old, he gave a brilliant interview. In fact, it lasted for two hours. As I said goodbye, I thought, "Here's to you, my friend. You really are the King of Comedy."

December of 2010 was incredibly busy. I shot most of the events that happened in the city. The month began with the NASCAR Victory Lap. The top 12 drivers were introduced in front of the Planet Hollywood hotel, which is where I was positioned. Then, they drove their race cars down the Las Vegas Strip. It was loud and exciting. On December 7th, I shot the NFR rodeo at Thomas & Mack. The News Bureau had some great new cameras, so it was a pleasure using one of them. I was able to capture the action indoors with great clarity. I was with Mayor Goodman on

December 8th when he lit the official Las Vegas Christmas Tree on Fremont Street. It was a colorful and cheerful evening. On the morning of December 15th, the Cosmopolitan hotel opened. I was there for the ribbon cutting. Getting fourteen people in the shot was rather challenging, but I did it. The Las Vegas Bowl football game took place on a cold and rainy December 22nd. Boise State defeated Utah 26-3. The afternoon started with a robust flyover by an Air Force F-22 Raptor, a Stealth air superiority fighter. Its speed and power were unbelievable. The event ended with the trophy presentation to the winning team. Besides the action, I shot a lot of ceremonial events that happened during the television commercials. The December events are good for our Southern Nevada economy. It's a great time of year for Las Vegas.

Because I have such a great relationship with Oscar Goodman, I think it's time to tell a few stories. The morning of August 3rd, 2010, began as a normal day in the office. I sat at my computer, editing photos and catching up on emails. However, the afternoon was quite different. At 12:30 p.m., I drove to City Hall for a 1:00 p.m. photo assignment. Much to my surprise, my wife, daughter, sister-in-law, and Rossi Ralenkotter were waiting for me. We were quickly escorted into the Mayor's office. Mayor Oscar B. Goodman welcomed us in his usual friendly manner, and we sat in the chairs which surrounded his desk. Oscar began talking about the city and then pointed out some of his memorabilia. He also told a few stories about the fascinating people who had visited him over the years. There were a few bottles of gin on his desk, one of which was called "Heather Gin." When he found out that my daughter's name was Heather, he gave her the bottle. She was thrilled, and everyone laughed. He then spoke about the importance of promoting Las Vegas through News Bureau photos. Surprisingly, the Mayor announced that I was to receive a proclamation from the city. He picked up a dark blue folder with the official seal embossed on the front. He read the proclamation out loud and then handed it to me. Much to my delight, he also gave me The Key to the City. Glenn Pinkerton, another News Bureau photographer, captured the moment with some memorable photos, and the event concluded. It was a very nice occasion to share with my family and friends.

A year later, Oscar moved into the Public Relations building of the Las Vegas Convention Center. Because of term limits, he was no longer the Mayor. Oscar Goodman's new title was "Chairman of the Las Vegas Host Committee." I was happy that he joined our team. I suddenly had the opportunity to talk to him every day. One afternoon, he told me that he was opening a new restaurant in the Plaza Hotel called "Oscar's." He wanted a taste of old Las Vegas and asked me if I could find the recipe for the once-famous Alpine Village soup. Believe it or not, we had a copy of the recipe at home. I gave the recipe to him, and he added it to the menu.

For my 64th birthday, Debbie and I went to Oscar's restaurant for dinner. I talked to Oscar earlier in the week and made sure he would be there that night. It was a classy restaurant with great food and a tremendous view of downtown Las Vegas. Because former Mayor Oscar Goodman was now sharing the Public Affairs building with me, we started most morning conversations with stories about the great days in Las Vegas. In fact, I would begin talking about a certain restaurant, and he would tell me his favorite dish or a story about the eatery. It became a fun way to begin each day. The time I mentioned the Aku Aku in the Stardust, Oscar said, "Not all the bugs were in the food." These conversations lasted until I finally ran out of places to mention.

At one point, Oscar told me that he was writing his autobiography entitled "BEING OSCAR." As time passed, he kept me posted on the book's progress. Finally, it was complete. One morning, he asked me to meet him at the "Welcome to Fabulous Las Vegas" sign with my camera. As I arrived, Oscar was already there with a martini glass and his two favorite showgirls. I knew it was to be a photo shoot but didn't know that it would become the cover of his book. We took some photos and returned to the office. A few months later, the book was published, and the cover looked beautiful.

Over the years, I attended dozens of events with Mayor Goodman. We were together at hospitals, sporting events, ribbon cuttings, and everything else you can imagine. He has always treated me with respect, as he does everyone. He may not be the best athlete when it comes to throwing out the first pitch at a baseball game, but he is a real gentleman. During an event at Cashman Field, I was talking to him about the early days in Las Vegas. I told him that my mom often mentioned Dave Berman, Moe Dalitz, and Ben Goffstein. With a slight smile and a twinkle in his eyes, he said, "They came with a little baggage."

I spent the morning of March 17th, 2011, photographing bagpipers on the Brooklyn Bridge in front of New York-New York. It was Saint Patrick's Day in Las Vegas. The music was actually very good, and the characters were colorful. Oscar Goodman was elected Grand Marshal for the event and gave a rousing speech. After that, I went to the Forum Shops and took pictures of the same group marching their way through the mall. As usual, I captured some interesting shots. There's no place like Las Vegas for special events. The next day, I was with Oscar once again. This time we were on Fremont Street promoting the Knight Rider Festival, a Paul Casey production honoring the long-running television show. Paul is also a fraternity brother from California. There were seventeen black Knight Rider cars escorting different celebrities to the stage. Showgirls danced in the street while Rossi, Oscar, and Paul gave speeches. I never thought much about the KITT cars until I looked inside one of them. The dashboard looked like a jet. It had more gadgets than I could imagine and a very fancy steering wheel. I returned to the office at about 7:00 p.m. and sent a picture of the showgirls to AP. Such is the life of a photographer.

Near the end of March 2011, I attended a preview of the Las Vegas Mob Experience at the Tropicana hotel. It was an interactive attraction that chronicled the rise and fall of organized crime in Las Vegas. It housed fascinating artifacts from the mobsters of the 1940s and 1950s. It was also a live game, where the patrons were part of the story. My mob name was "Potatoes." I had to be alert and not get arrested. That day was actually a press event, and special guests were in attendance. I met many of the mobster's relatives. Even though Al Capone's grandson was there, I spent most of my time talking to Bugsy Siegel's daughter, Millicent. After all, our parents knew each other. I told her the story of how mom asked Mr. Siegel if she could work in the pit, and she told me some stories about her dad. Suddenly, I had a new friend. We kept the conversation family-oriented and left out the mob hits. It was another interesting day to be a native Las Vegan.

A couple of days after my encounter with the mobsters, I photographed Michael Jordan during a press conference at Shadow Creek golf course. He was promoting the Michael Jordan Celebrity Invitational, a charity tournament. The press conference was held outside, and I captured some pictures of the course while we waited for Michael. When he arrived, he had golf clubs, so I presumed he was going to practice before the tournament. He answered questions and seemed very professional. The next day was the tournament. I arrived at Shadow Creek at 7:00 a.m. and walked to the first tee. I photographed Roger Clemens, Wayne Gretzky, Ken Griffey, Jr., John Smoltz, Mike Piazza, and Michael Jordan. They were all very good golfers. If they were not, they wouldn't embarrass themselves by playing in a tournament. Even though other sports celebrities were there, I had what I needed and returned to work. I sent the images to the wires and called it a day. Walking around a beautiful golf course with a camera is a nice way to make a living.

In May 2011, Las Vegas hosted the Global Travel & Tourism Summit. It was a gathering of travel and tourism leaders held at the Aria Resort & Casino. Of the three-day conference, one event stood out as the most interesting. A select group of people was to greet Felipe Calderon, the President of Mexico, in the green room. I was the only photographer allowed to attend. Our group consisted of David Scowsill, President/CEO WTTC; Rossi Ralenkotter, President/CEO LVCVA; Bill McBeath, President/COO ARIA; Geoffrey Kent, Chairman WTTC, Oscar B. Goodman, Mayor of Las Vegas and Mrs. Goodman. Because President Calderon was a visiting head of state, he was accompanied by the Secret Service. He also had his own security force, which added a different dimension. They wanted to know who everyone was, including the Mayor. Things got interesting in a hurry. At first, we were told to wait in the hallway. Then we were told to go into the green room. A few minutes later, we were moved back to the hallway. Right before Mr. Calderon arrived, we were escorted back into the green room. At that point, Mayor Goodman looked at me but didn't say anything. We just went along with the program. Finally, the President walked into the room, and I started taking candid shots. He shook hands with the dignitaries and engaged in conversation. I thought Mr. Calderon was charismatic and dignified. The meet and greet lasted about twenty minutes, and then we left the area. I went back to my photo position in the great hall while everyone else went their separate ways. Soon, President Calderon appeared on stage and gave an interesting speech on tourism in his country. All in all, the Summit was a great success. It had very high-profile speakers, such as Secretary of Transportation Ray LaHood and Secretary of the Department of Homeland Security Janet Napolitano. I was proud of my hometown for hosting a world-class event.

I traveled a couple of times for business in 2012. Rossi was appointed Chair of the United States Travel and Tourism Advisory Board for the United States Department of Commerce. We wanted to document the occasion, so I traveled to Washington, D.C., to attend a tourism press conference and take photos. It was a rather sophisticated event with members of Congress and tourism officials in attendance. Because the famous cherry blossoms were in bloom, I also took some great photos of our group with the Jefferson Memorial in the background.

My next trip was to the Los Angeles Convention Center to attend Pow Wow, an annual gathering of international journalists. Las Vegas sponsored an event, and I captured it with my trusty Nikon. This was a quick trip. I was there and back the same day.

Because Rossi and I attended Saint Joseph School at the same time, we decided to return to the campus in 2012 and take some pictures. Glenn was there to take photos, and Heather accompanied us for moral support. We took some photos outside, and then we moved into a classroom and finished our shoot. While we were there, we met the principal. He was also a lifelong resident of Las Vegas. It was a fun day.

On March 30th, 2012, I photographed Holly Madison in a room at the Las Vegas Convention Center. The News Bureau wanted to re-create the famous Miss Atomic Bomb photo that Don English took in 1957, and we chose Holly to pose for it. I took the shot in an air-conditioned room that had bright lights and a green background. The image was then put on the same black-and-white background as the original picture. I thought it turned out very well.

May 5-13, 2012, was Travel and Tourism Week. I was interviewed by Fox 5 regarding the 65th Anniversary of the Las Vegas News Bureau and how our photos relate to Travel and Tourism. The segment ran on Fox 5 in the morning and continued to run on Fox's MORE ACCESS show in the evening at 6 p.m. The reporter, Claudine Grant, was in the News Bureau for an hour and did a very good job. The story was both informative and interesting. Somehow, I looked pretty good on television.

Wednesday of the same week, the News Bureau anniversary luncheon was held at the Las Vegas Convention Center. It was a wonderful event, with a lot of surprises. Paula Francis was the Master of Ceremonies. Rossi made a speech, Holly Madison was introduced as the new Miss Atomic Bomb, and the News Bureau employees were applauded. We were treated to lunch and a historical video. We also took a group photo with Holly. The next day I was shooting an event at Aria called "Leadership Las Vegas." As I walked in, they were showing the same video that was played at the anniversary luncheon. Gordon Absher suddenly called me up to the stage and interviewed me regarding the history of the News Bureau. I tried not to panic as he asked about some of my favorite assignments. I was taken by surprise and was not ready for another interview, especially in front of a live audience. Somehow, I struggled through it. In the end, I was happy that Tourism Week was winding down.

On June 27th, 2012, I spent the entire day at McCarran International Airport. The new Terminal 3 was opened, and I photographed all of the festivities. Besides the arrivals of Virgin Atlantic and British Air, Governor Brian Sandoval, Rossi Ralenkotter, and Randy Walker were subjects of my camera. I worked into the night because of a gala reception and took photos of the invited guests.

For me, August 15th, 2012, was an early morning photo shoot. I went to Town Square to document the ribbon cutting of a $246.5 million redesign of Interstate 15 South. The six-mile project stretched from Tropicana Avenue to just south of Silverado Ranch Boulevard. The project included widening the freeway, adding northbound and southbound access roads, redesigning five interchanges, and building 26 new bridge sections, 35 retaining walls, and sound walls. Once again, Rossi and the Governor were in attendance. It was hot and sunny, but we all made it through the speeches. Afterward, Governor Sandoval gave me the secret fraternity handshake. I stopped at Starbucks on the way back to the office.

In 2011, Caesars Entertainment began construction on the world's tallest observation wheel. It was to be called "The High Roller." Not to be confused with a Ferris wheel, it would become a moving wheel that featured 28 spherical cabins, which would accommodate up to 40 passengers each. Located next to the Flamingo and across the street from Caesars Palace, it would make quite a splash on Las Vegas Boulevard. I started photographing the construction from the beginning and continued until it was finished. Every few months, I would go to the same vacant lot on Koval Lane and document the construction process. It finally opened in the spring of 2014. At 550 feet tall, it was spectacular. On media day, I was invited to ride the wheel. After a ribbon-cutting ceremony, I climbed aboard and started taking photos. The journey lasted 30 minutes. It was a nice view of the Strip and a very smooth ride. I'm sure the scenery looks a lot different at night. It has become a great addition to Las Vegas.

Toward the end of my career, PBS decided to produce a segment on the News Bureau. A television crew came to the office. They spent the day filming the archival photos and interviewing me. They also wanted to follow me on a photo assignment. The New Year's Eve fireworks were approaching, so we planned that event for the video shoot. When the day came, we all gathered in the lobby of the Trump Tower. We were escorted to the roof at 11:30 p.m. and set up our equipment. At the stroke of midnight, the fireworks shot into the air. I photographed the fireworks, and the PBS crew filmed me. Sometime later, the PBS special was on the air. It was picked up by several PBS affiliates across the country. I thought it looked really good and was very proud to be a part of the production.

In the spring of 2014, there was a celebration of life in downtown Las Vegas. A "Life Cube" was to be burned in a vacant lot near Fremont Street. People were encouraged to write down their goals, dreams, wishes, and aspirations and place them in the cube. The cube would then be burned, and their wishes would rise toward the heavens. I had taken pictures of the cube being built, so my curiosity helped me drive to the location. I arrived early and looked for a good vantage point to take the photos. Directly across the street from the lot was a bar named "Atomic Liquors." I didn't know it at the time, but that particular bar was the oldest bar in Las Vegas. I went inside and asked if I could take pictures from their roof. Surprisingly, they said yes. I grabbed my camera and tripod from my car and then climbed a ladder up to the roof. I shared the roof with a couple of other photographers. They were very courteous, and we all prepared for the ceremony. When the time came, the crowds below gathered around the cube, and the speeches began. Soon, someone lit the cube. I took some very beautiful photos during the process. It turned out to be a pleasant experience. It reminded me of a high school bonfire. The crowds were quiet and peaceful, the night air was warm, and I had a great time. After it was over, I drove back to the office and sent the photos out. News assignments can be very intense. This one was an exception. It was actually quite fun.

August 20th, 2014 was the 50th anniversary of The Beatles' only Las Vegas appearance. They played two concerts at the convention center. Therefore, the executive team decided to celebrate the event with festivities of our own. During the year, the News Bureau taped interviews with people who attended the concerts. I was one of them. My interview took place at the Golden Gate, where I got my tickets. All of the interviews were presented on a monitor in the convention center lobby, along with photos of the Beatles. Our event was actually held on August 12th because we wanted the Board Members to attend after their monthly meeting. During the celebration, speeches were made, photos were taken, and a commemorative plaque was unveiled on a wall near Starbucks Coffee. The ones who attended the concerts were given lanyards that said, "I was there." I took some pictures, and I was also in some pictures. It was a relaxing day at the convention center.

October 17th, 2014, was my last photo shoot for the Las Vegas News Bureau. It was the day I retired. Rossi was being honored with a tourism award, so most of the employees gathered in front of the convention center at 11:00 a.m. to congratulate him. He had another engagement and was not at work that day. I was in a cherry picker and lifted about 25 feet into the air. I took the group shot with a

Nikon D800. I shared the moment with a video person from R&R Partners. After the shoot, I walked back to the office for the final time. I downloaded the images into my computer and called it a day. After work, a few co-workers gathered at a dive bar down the street called "Davy's Locker." We had some drinks, and they wished me well in retirement. It was a simple way to end a wonderful career. My job was very special. I loved promoting Las Vegas.

Because of my retirement, I was featured in the June 2015 edition of Desert Companion online magazine. The article was entitled "Fire in the sky: images of an ever-changing Strip." They showed some of the photos that I had taken over the course of my News Bureau career. Seeing the photos again helped me appreciate what a great job I had as a photojournalist. I'll never forget those special moments.

Chapter 6: Golden Nuggets

Debbie Guilbault and I were married at Saint Genevieve Catholic Church in Panorama City, California, on January 19, 1974. After the reception, we drove to San Luis Obispo. The Madonna Inn was the first stop on our honeymoon. It was a unique place to stay. The rooms were beautiful, as was the countryside. Our next stop was in San Francisco. We stayed at a hotel near Fisherman's Wharf. Knowing that our final stop would be Lake Tahoe, we bought snow boots at a sporting goods store in the city. When we arrived at the south shore of the lake, there was plenty of snow. Purchasing the boots suddenly became a great investment. Those snow boots were so well made that I used them for thirty years. We enjoyed our honeymoon very much. In fact, we took another road trip six months later. This time, we drove to the Florida Keys. Now that's a road trip.

The year I graduated from Gorman, the most popular television shows were "Bonanza" and "My Three Sons." The best music groups were The Mamas and Papas, Simon and Garfunkel, the Beatles, and The Beach Boys. The price of a movie ticket was about $1.70. I remember seeing "The Sound of Music" at the Fremont theater downtown. I wouldn't have gone to a musical, but it was a date movie. I forget who I took; it was probably Shirley Russo. Naturally, real men like me only went to Steve McQueen movies.

I always loved baseball, and I was pretty good at it. Most

people do not continue playing the game after their youth, but somehow I found a way to stay active in the sport. It was called an adult softball league. I played center field for Shifty's, a neighborhood bar across the street from Wonder World on West Sahara Avenue. It all started one night when a bunch of guys was having drinks. The conversation got around to baseball, so we decided to form a team. As we talked among ourselves, we learned that most of us were good players. Some of the guys were more than good; they were All-State in high school. We were still in our prime and decided to give it a go. We asked Shifty's to sponsor us. It was normal for bars to provide T-shirts and pay an entrance fee for the softball league. In return, we gave them our business after the games. Everybody was happy. Our team was made up of guys from Western High School, Gorman High School, and the Telephone Company. Most of us had goofy personalities, so we were a good mix. We didn't take anything seriously, and we played like the rag-tag teams from the early days of baseball. It was a deadly combination for the teams that played against us. We only lost a couple of games that year. I played on several teams after that, but none were as much fun or as good as Shifty's team.

That same year, I played on an adult flag football team in Reno. If I hadn't been in such good shape, I would not have survived the bitterly cold weather. We asked Pizza Hut to sponsor us, and they were happy to do it. We made the same deal with them as with Shifty's. After the games, we went to the restaurant for pizza. I was one of the running backs, and Frank Rosta was the other. We were a couple of Gorman guys who played together in the outfield for Shifty's a few months earlier. Dick Morris was our quarterback. He was a fraternity brother from Reno. We decided to pick the worst name possible, so we checked all the college mascots. We settled on "The Fighting Blue Hens." That was the name of the sports teams from the University of Delaware. The one thing Frank, Dick, and I had in common was the fact that we were small, fast, and a little cocky. Flag football is usually a passing game, but we were a running team because of our speed. We surprised everyone and won most of the games. We beat a lot of teams that were filled with big, slow guys. They were poor losers and usually wanted to fight after the games. Of course, it didn't help when we laughed at them.

My involvement in sports kept me active. Between scuba diving, golf, baseball, and football, I've had a very happy and healthy life. The coldest I have ever been while scuba diving happened in the waters of Lake Tahoe. Although I spent many hours in the lake, one particular day stands out. It was in January. I was young, so cold water didn't bother me. As I surfaced from the dive, I saw people skiing down the slopes of the Incline Village Ski Resort. I thought to myself, "What in the world are they doing up there when they could be in the water with me."

In the summer of 1992, I achieved the rating of Master Scuba Diver from PADI (Professional Association of Diving Instructors). It took many years and a lot of training, but I finally reached the certification. My prerequisite courses had names such as Rescue Diver, Underwater Navigator, Underwater Photographer, Equipment Specialist, and Advanced Open Water Diver. They were all fascinating, but one class stood out from the rest. It was called Drift Diving. For this event, the Colorado River was my classroom. After some technical instruction, my classmates and I were taken by boat to a spot below Hoover Dam. Once there, we donned our equipment and entered the water. The river was cold, but I was well prepared. I had a full wetsuit with a hood and gloves. Suddenly, the current surrounded us, and we began our journey. I couldn't believe the visibility. It was crystal clear, similar to Lake Tahoe. Along the river bottom, there were different species of fish hiding in the grass. We were told to look for Colorado Squawfish and Razorback Suckers. They were both listed as endangered. I saw a lot of fish that day. Maybe the Squawfish and Suckers were among them. I also had an eerie feeling they were watching me. We drifted for a couple of miles, and then the dive was over. On the surface, we climbed onto the boat and rode to Willow Beach. The next day, we did the same thing. It was a two-day open water class. The entire experience was marvelous.

I had Jury Duty twice. The first time was a criminal trial

regarding a woman cheating on slot machines. We found her guilty. The entire trial lasted one day. The second trial was a week of agony. A man fell in the bathroom of a Strip hotel and sued for damages. The first day was jury selection. It was an exhausting process, where each lawyer asked the prospective jurors personal questions. After they weeded out the undesirables, the final ten were selected. I was one of the chosen few who made the cut. In a civil trial, twelve jurors are not required. The opening arguments were presented, and then we were dismissed for the day. On the second day, the witnesses began to testify. It was Saint Patrick's Day, and I walked across the street to the Courthouse Bar & Grill for lunch. The trial started to get confusing at this point. Day three was stressful for all involved. The attorneys tried to discredit the witnesses. On day four, the injured party took the stand. He contradicted his written statements from seven years ago, and he was not coherent. At this point, I thought he was his own worst enemy. On the last day, both attorneys gave their final arguments. The jury deliberated for a short time and found in favor of the Defendant. Afterward, the judge briefed us. Then, both lawyers questioned us regarding the verdict. The judge was a fellow Bishop Gorman Alumni, so I felt comfortable. It was a very interesting process, but I was glad when it was finished. An entire week of anxiety was enough for me.

In November of 2003, I received terrible news. Bobby

Hatfield had passed away. It was such an empty and helpless feeling. All I could do was take a deep breath and try to remember the exceptional times we had. The best moments with Bobby were usually after the late shows. He just wanted to have a cocktail and some quiet conversation. During football season, we would get parlay cards from the casino and try to pick the winners. It was his way of unwinding. Bobby's funeral was one of the most emotional days of my life. It was more than sad; it was devastating. He was my hero, my fraternity brother, and my best friend, all rolled into one. When you lose your best friend, your life changes forever. All you have left are the memories. Bobby was a sensational entertainer with the voice of an angel. He was also a world-class human being.

After Bobby passed away, Bill went on tour for about a year with the Righteous Brothers band. As things changed, that tour also came to an end. His last show with the band was at the Orleans Hotel. They wanted me to photograph the performance from the audience's point of view. They also wanted a special shot of their final bow from the drum set. That was a great opportunity for me. When they took the final bow, I shot it from Dave's position on the drums. I was dressed in black like the members of the band, and the audience didn't notice that we had switched drummers. I took the photo, and it turned out wonderful. It was a very emotional moment for the band and me. It was time to say goodbye.

In 2005, Debbie and I went to the Cayman Islands for some great scuba diving and snorkeling. We flew Continental Airlines from Las Vegas to Houston, then to Grand Cayman. In case the pilot got lost, I was ready to tell him to go past Cuba and turn left. The island was easy to find. When we landed, I wanted to kiss the ground. I waited thirty years to get there, and I was very happy. In the past, I didn't have the time or the money. In 2005, I had both. We stayed at a resort called Sunset House, which was built for scuba divers. It had no sandy beach, just a rocky shore that dropped into the best diving spot on earth.

I had never seen anything like the beauty of the Cayman Islands. Because it was June, the air temperature was 84 degrees, and the water temperature was the same. For me, it was perfect. There was a sign posted in our bathroom that said the water was safe to drink. At that point, I knew I was in Heaven. One day, we drove to a part of the island called Hell. While there, I took a picture of the devil. He was about three feet tall. I guess you could say we went to Heaven and Hell on the same trip. Sunset House is the home base of a world-famous underwater photographer named Cathy Church. She has a nice photography store on the grounds. During the week, we spent a few hours talking to her. She had a parrot named Sparky that lived in the shop. I rented an underwater camera from her on the day we went to Stingray City. Yes, I went scuba diving with stingrays. There were about twenty of those strange creatures that lived on a shallow sand bar. While the other divers were feeding them, I knelt on the sandy bottom and photographed the graceful animals. I figured that they didn't have teeth, so they wouldn't bite. Anyway, as I took pictures, the stingrays would slowly glide over me and look for some food. A couple of them tried to land on my head, so I brushed them away. The males weren't very big, but the females were four feet across. During the week, I went scuba diving at other locations, but Stingray City was the cream of the crop. There was a famous mermaid statue located in thirty-five feet of water at Sunset Reef, right behind Sunset House. I went diving near the statue one day with an employee of Cathy's photography store. He took pictures of me with the statue. On the same dive, we found a small barge at seventy feet and took more pictures. It was nice to have my picture taken for a change. Each time Debbie and I got into the water, we saw brightly colored fish called Parrot Fish. They had a parrot-like beak, which they used to scrape algae from coral and rocks. Once in the water, we could hear them scraping. It was a unique experience. One day, Debbie made friends with a rather large barracuda. The fish must have liked her because it followed her for a while. In her case, I don't think the feeling was mutual. Sunset House had a great open-air restaurant where we ate our meals. It was right next to the Caribbean Sea. The food was great, and the employees were from many different countries. During the evening, most of the hotel guests gathered at the bar and talked about their underwater discoveries. It was a magnificent vacation.

As I watched one of the new Batman movies, I thought of the time I met the original Batman, Adam West. He was at the opening of Masquerade Village Casino at the Rio hotel. During the same event, I ran into my old friend Nancy Sinatra, and we had a short visit. Anyway, Adam was everything you would hope he would be. He was relaxed, cordial, and very cool. I also had another encounter with the Batman series. Warner Brothers Studio was modernizing the Batmobile, and they scheduled a press conference at the Desert Inn golf course. They hired me for the event, and I photographed the new Batmobile. Before I left for the evening, I had to give them the film. They considered it their property. It was top secret because the movie was still in production. Nobody was allowed to see the car at that time.

I attended a great party after "Footloose" at the Rio. This time, my daughter, Heather, went with me. Actually, it was the best party of all time. Kevin Bacon and the Bacon Brothers band performed. They were very mellow, and everyone was relaxed. The food was fabulous. It always was at the Rio. They didn't hold back on anything. Heather really enjoyed herself. She rested her arms on the stage and listened to the music. All of the usual suspects were there. I called them the usual suspects because they were the ones who attended all the parties and received the free gifts. Oh no, I became one of them.

A local's favorite restaurant was called the Green Shack. It was located next to the Showboat hotel and was famous for fried chicken. The Shack was small and simple, but so was Las Vegas. I went there a few times with my parents and really enjoyed it. While working for the News Bureau, I photographed the closing of a famous eatery. As I entered the door for the final time, the owners were putting away the frying pans and the recipe books. It was a sad day. I felt as if a part of my family history was also closing.

The year was 2006. Debbie and I went to Reno to see the University of Nevada play Northwestern University in football. It wasn't Homecoming, but it was the first time the Wolf Pack played a Big Ten school. We ordered our tickets online, and away we went. That weekend, there was a motorcycle rally that took over the entire city. There wasn't one room available in town, so we stayed at a resort near Lake Tahoe called Northstar. The ballgame was played at night, which meant we had to drive back to the lake through a dark forest. As for the game, the Wolf Pack beat the Wildcats 31 to 21. September was a great time of year to be in northern Nevada because the summer crowds were gone. The next day, we drove to Sand Harbor and walked along the shore. It was a strange feeling. Nobody was there. The autumn foliage and the pine-scented air created a perfect afternoon. Even though the Ponderosa Ranch had been sold and the Cartwright family was gone, it was still a great trip.

Every once in a while, I've had a day that I placed on my "Greatest Day Ever" list. One such day happened in 2007. We were in Hawaii on a family vacation. I booked a scuba and snorkel adventure on the Pride of Maui, a beautiful sixty-five-foot catamaran. At first, the five-hour trip sounded like a long time. Boy, was I wrong. It went by so quickly that I wanted to do it all over again the next day. We boarded the boat at 8:00 a.m. and enjoyed a continental breakfast on the way to Molokini Crater. When we arrived at our destination, the passengers got into the water. Some of us went scuba diving, while the others snorkeled. My dive lasted about fifty minutes. I rented an underwater camera and saw a wide variety of fish. Debbie and Heather had a great time snorkeling. On our way to the next stop, the crew barbecued hamburgers and chicken. They also offered us salad and fruit. We built up quite an appetite, so the lunch tasted great. Our second stop was at Turtle Town. It was a place where large Hawaiian Green Sea Turtles lived among the underwater lava formations. We jumped back into the water and continued our adventure. The turtles were very large and moved slowly. I tried to maneuver myself in front of them to capture the right photo, but they stayed just out of reach. It became a game of cat and mouse, and I lost. I only got pictures of their rear ends. The water was warm, but not like the water in the Caribbean. On the way back to the harbor, they played the music of the Beach Boys. At 1:00 p.m., we docked, and our adventure was over. The crew was friendly, the food was good, and the boat ride was smooth. It was one of the greatest days ever.

One of my most sentimental moments unfolded at Bishop Gorman High School. It was not an official assignment for the News Bureau, but I took my camera anyway. The last basketball game in the old Gorman gymnasium was to be played that night, and I attended the game as an alumnus. I snapped a few pictures of the state championship banners hanging from the ceiling and the people in the stands. It was a great send-off for The House of Glory. The campus was teaming with life. To me, it seemed like yesterday, even though it had been forty years since my graduation.

I used to follow professional football more than I do now. In fact, I was a Dallas Cowboys fanatic. During the 1970s, the Cowboys held training camps at California Lutheran College in Thousand Oaks. The team trained in California because the summers in Texas were very hot and humid. Cal Lutheran was a short drive from Las Vegas, so I began traveling to camp each August. At first, I took photos from the bleachers like everyone else. I soon discovered that the atmosphere was more casual than the regular season, so I decided to get closer to the players. After many conversations with Coach Tom Landry and defensive coordinator Ernie Stautner, I was allowed on the field. I shot the workouts, the scrimmages, and the drills. I took most of my photos from the sidelines, but once in a while, I was allowed to shoot from the tower. I remember taking pictures of Tony Dorsett during his rookie year. He had masking tape on the front of his helmet with his name. Everyone knew who he was, but it was a rookie tradition.

Training camp was tough for the players. There were two practices a day, one at 9:00 a.m. and another at 3:00 p.m. Their time was tightly controlled. Breakfast was from 7:00 to 8:00 a.m., lunch was from 12:00 to 1:00 p.m., and dinner was from 6:00 to 7:00 p.m. They ended each day with a meeting from 7:30 to 10:00 p.m. It was an exciting time to interact with the Cowboy players. With names like Roger Staubach, Too Tall Jones, Charlie Waters, Cliff Harris, and Lee Roy Jordan, the team was loaded with talent. I had to squeeze in my conversations whenever I could, usually while they walked from the practice field to the dorms. For some reason, Randy White and Harvey Martin became my pals. I liked their personalities. They were confident and talented but humble. They were also part of the Dallas

Cowboys' Doomsday defense, which was really Tom Landry's Flex defense. At one point during training camp, people were invited to have a barbecue dinner with the team. That was one event I couldn't miss. Picnic tables were set up on a grassy area near the dorms, and fans enjoyed dining with their favorite players. Debbie and I couldn't cut into the steaks with the plastic silverware that was provided, so we began to bring our own. In fact, we brought a lot of silverware. Suddenly, the players wanted to sit with us. I asked Harvey Martin if he liked eating with the fans. He said it was great, and he looked forward to it. One time, Robert Newhouse sat at our table and actually cleaned the silverware before he returned it to Debbie. The picnic was always quite a scene. The fans wore Cowboy jerseys, while the players dressed in golf shirts. All in all, I made my annual pilgrimage to training camp eleven years in a row. Each one was a unique experience. It was a very special part of my life.

Early in 2010, Heather purchased a Dallas Cowboys commemorative brick. It was actually a personalized paver that was placed on a walkway outside the new football stadium. It was engraved with the letters "Go Cowboys Darrin Debbie & Heather Bush." We decided to visit our brick, so we booked a trip to Dallas for the Thanksgiving Day game against the New Orleans Saints. Our sports package included three nights at a great hotel called the

Gaylord Texan. It was a cross between the Bellagio and the Ponderosa Ranch. The hotel was decorated for the Christmas holiday and was very festive. Upon our arrival, we had a buffet dinner with three players, two cheerleaders, and five hundred complete strangers. The next day, we were transported to the stadium by bus. It was snowing, but we were determined to find our brick. After looking at thousands of bricks, we found ours. We took pictures with it and entered the stadium. The tailgate party was out of the question. There was something about eating frozen hotdogs that didn't sound very good. To our delight, it was warm inside. The game was exciting, and the fans were more than enthusiastic. We wore Cowboy jerseys and cheered like crazy. It didn't help the home team; they lost. After the game, we returned to the hotel for a turkey dinner. The next day, we went back to Cowboys Stadium for a walking tour. We saw the locker rooms, took pictures on the field, and spent too much money in the gift shop. It was a great trip. I must admit, it seems a little strange to plan your vacation around a brick.

Debbie, Heather, and I traveled to San Diego for spring break in March of 2010. We stayed at the Marriott Hotel and Marina, which is next door to the convention center. We like the hotel because of its location. It's within walking distance of some of our favorite restaurants. During the trip, we went to the zoo and walked through the Gaslamp Quarter, which is a 16-block historical neighborhood downtown. The zoo was splendid because a lot of baby animals were on display. One morning, we took a boat ride on the bay. It was narrated, so we learned a lot about history. The United States Navy has a huge presence in San Diego, and we saw most of it. Our tour boat slowly passed shipyards that were filled with destroyers. We also saw the USS Nimitz and the USS Ronald Reagan, two nuclear-powered supercarriers. The USS Nimitz (CVN-68) was commissioned in 1975. The USS Ronald Reagan (CVN-76) was commissioned in 2003. Both ships were very impressive, to say the least. We felt proud and safe. Although I took hundreds of pictures at the zoo, the ones of the Koalas came out the best. They were actually awake.

June 13, 2010, was a wonderful day. Debbie, Heather, and I attended a horserace at Hollywood Park. We had been following the career of an undefeated horse named Zenyatta, so we couldn't resist the temptation to see her in action. To our good fortune, it was Zenyatta bobblehead day at the track. Heather made reservations for us at the Turf Club, so we dressed in our best Sunday clothes. We met Debbie's brother and his daughters at the gate, where we picked up our bobbleheads. We then proceeded to the Turf Club and were escorted to our table. As time passed, we bet on a few horses, ate lunch at the buffet, and bought some souvenirs. Before the big race, we walked down to the paddock area to see Zenyatta up close. Everyone else had the same idea; the area was packed. Suddenly, Zenyatta entered the arena, and the applause started. Soon after that, her jockey, Mike Smith, climbed aboard. They passed right in front of us on their way to the track. We then walked quickly back to our seats to see the race. The horses were put into the starting gate, and the race began. Zenyatta was running last for most of the race. Suddenly, she began to overtake horse after horse. Entering the final turn, Zenyatta hunted down St Trinians and passed her by a half-length to win the 69th Vanity Handicap and set a record for modern-day top-tier thoroughbreds with her 17th consecutive victory. After the race, the Hall of Fame jockey walked her to the center of the track, where they proudly stood and absorbed the thunderous applause. For us, it was the end of a glorious day. For Zenyatta, it was a job well done. At six years old, she was still undefeated.

The University of Nevada football team had a phenomenal year in 2010. In fact, it was the best in the history of the program. They ended up with a record of 12 wins and one loss. They were the co-champions of the WAC Conference and were invited to play in the Kraft Fight Hunger Bowl in San Francisco's AT&T Park on January 9, 2011. I needed to go to that game, so I put Heather in charge of the tickets. We arrived in San Francisco on Saturday, January 8, and checked into the Saint Francis hotel. We then walked to Chinatown and had lunch at the Oriental Pearl, a great restaurant. After lunch, we did some shopping. Heather wanted to wear something blue to the game, so she bought a blue wig in one of the gift shops. After that, we walked to the Embarcadero and joined a Nevada pep rally at Gordon Biersch. We continued our journey to AT&T Park to buy a few World Series baseball souvenirs. That night, Mike Smithwick joined us at a famous San Francisco restaurant named John's Grill. On Sunday morning, there was a large pep rally in Union Square. The momentum was building toward the big game. Heather and I ate lunch at Lefty O'Doul's and then took the Municipal Railway (Muni) to the ballpark. We met Mike at the Willie Mays statue and walked inside. I loved the fact that a football game was being played in a baseball stadium. I wore my Wolf Pack jersey, Heather wore her blue hair, and Mike wore his Sundowner hat. We asked someone to take a picture of us, and it became an instant classic. It was one of the best photos of the night. It wasn't an action shot, but it was very colorful. There were four SAEs at the game, Chris Ault (the Wolf Pack Coach), Brian Sandoval (the Governor of Nevada), Mike, and me. The game was very exciting, and Nevada beat Boston College 20 – 13. After the hard-fought victory, we walked onto the field with the rest of the 41,000 fans and joined the celebration. At about 10:30 p.m., we took the train back to Powell Street and walked to our hotel. The next day, Heather went ice skating on the rink at Union Square. Later in the afternoon, we flew home. It was a wonderful trip.

To celebrate the summer of 2011, Mike Cortney and I decided to play golf at Pebble Beach. Debbie and I flew Allegiant Airlines to Monterey, rented a car, and drove to Carmel. We stayed at Clint Eastwood's Mission Ranch, a century-old dairy farm that he turned into a bed and breakfast. The next day, we met Mike and Julie at the Pebble Beach Golf Course. We had an early lunch and proceeded to the first tee. Mike was ready; he had played the course before. I felt like a lamb heading to slaughter. We then hit our drives, and the journey began. I was in trouble right away but came too far to quit. Besides, I was wearing the best-looking pants on the course. It was a magnificent day. Debbie took some pictures, and I managed to par two holes. Pebble Beach is like Golf Heaven. Between the morning fog, the ocean breeze, and the beauty of the course, it's as good as it gets. I hope to play there again. The next day, we took a drive to see the other courses owned by Pebble Beach Resorts. The Links at Spanish Bay and Spyglass Hill are also world-class golf courses on the ocean. I bought a shirt from both of them. That night, a bagpiper played music on the first tee at Spanish Bay. I believe it's a Scottish tradition to end each day with music. It was quite a sight. During our trip, we walked on the beach at Carmel, hiked through the forest at Point Lobos, and saw a lot of wildlife. The trip was much more than I expected.

The Sahara hotel was scheduled to close on May 16,

2011. When I heard the news, I called Sandy Hackett. The News Bureau wanted to interview people who had a history with the hotel, and I suggested Sandy. He came to the office on a Tuesday afternoon, and I introduced him to the staff. It was great to see him again after so many years. As he began the video interview, I was amazed at how much he remembered. He worked in several different departments, from Food and Beverage to Entertainment, so he had a lot of stories. Because he was there the same years that I was, I understood everything he said. His stories were fascinating and made me realize how much I enjoyed working at the Sahara. In those days, I was young and had a lot of enthusiasm. Sandy talked for more than an hour. After that, he left to perform in his own show at the Riviera called "Sandy Hackett's Rat Pack Show." For me, it was another very enjoyable day at work.

One year, I made a suggestion to Mayor Oscar Goodman to give the Key to the City to the Righteous Brothers. They had a long and successful history with Las Vegas, and I felt they deserved it. Long story short, the process took so long that Bobby had already died. Finally, there was a press conference at the Orleans, and Mayor Goodman presented Bill with the key. Afterward, I thanked the Mayor for his time and told him that Bill really enjoyed it. I thought that Bobby should also have been given a key and that Linda should have received it on his behalf. After all, they were the

Righteous Brothers.

One of Bobby and Bill's wishes was to get inducted into the Rock And Roll Hall Of Fame. Their names were mentioned for many years, but nobody seemed to pay attention to them. Suddenly, it became my mission to give it a try. One day, I found the name of the publicist for the Hall Of Fame, and we started corresponding. I nominated them, and the process began to unfold. I then contacted Dick Lies, the Executive Director of the SAE fraternity. I suggested that we collect signatures on a petition at the next fraternity convention and submit the document to the Hall Of Fame. During the convention, we collected hundreds of signatures. After that, we put the official seal of the fraternity on the papers and sent it away. I then called the publicist to make sure that she received it. Then it became a waiting game. About a year later, Bobby told me that they were going to be inducted into the Rock And Roll Hall Of Fame. I was extremely happy for them. Nobody will remember that it was SAE that put the icing on the cake with the petition. All that matters is that Bobby's wishes came true before he passed away.

I was driving to work early one morning on Desert Inn Road, and the sun rose over the hotels on the Strip. All I could see were their silhouettes because of the haze in the sky. As I looked at the many different structures, I couldn't help but think of the way life used to be in my hometown.

Las Vegas was a gambling town, but it was small, quiet, and sophisticated. People dressed up when they went out. The casinos were quiet by today's standards, and the hotels were a lot smaller. I remember going to the Desert Inn with my parents to see the headliners in the Crystal Room. We usually attended the dinner shows. I was too young for the cocktail shows. Dad wore a coat and tie, and mom was dressed in diamonds and furs. I was dressed in my best sport coat and displayed my best manners.

I knew two members of the Rat Pack, Joey Bishop and Sammy Davis Jr. I met Sammy backstage at the Desert Inn in the 1980s. We took Heather there to say hello and take some pictures. One of his big songs was "The Candy Man," so he had giant bowls of candy in his dressing room. Heather ate some and took a bag of assorted chocolates home. Sammy spent most of his time playing cards with the stagehands between shows. That's how he relaxed.

Many years after Frank Sinatra was in the audience at the Sahara, I photographed his last show at the Desert Inn. It was also one of the last times he appeared in Las Vegas. I stood in the back of the room with a long lens and snapped pictures of Old Blue Eyes. It was thrilling to see a real legend perform.

I have always been a Shirley MacLaine fan. I photographed her show at the Desert Inn, and I was there when she received an award from a woman's group at the

D.I. Country Club. But I actually got to talk to Shirley at Caesars Palace. One night, there was a formal gala that Shirley attended. I wanted to give her an archival picture of herself and have her sign another one for the News Bureau. Because there were so many people, I couldn't get close to her. Then, I had an idea. I simply held up the picture, and she saw it. She left whatever conversation she was having and came over to me. We talked about the picture, and she was glad to autograph it.

Over the years, I've learned that entertainers love to see pictures of themselves. In 1999, Johnny Rivers appeared at the Silverton. I found an archival News Bureau photo of him on stage at the Aladdin in 1979 and took it to his show. After the performance, Debbie and I went backstage and gave him the picture. He loved it and was glad to sign it. He didn't want to misspell Bureau, so I prompted him. At least he made sure that it was done right. He was a musician who appeared in town many times and appreciated someone thinking of him.

The original Helldorado parades were held on Fremont Street. They started in 1935, as part of the Helldorado Days celebration. Along with the parades were rodeos, and a carnival called Helldorado Village. It was a community event, where everyone dressed in western apparel. It was also my introduction to snow cones and cotton candy. There were three parades; the Old Timers Parade, the Kiddies

Parade, and the Beauty Parade. The floats were elaborate, and usually had showroom entertainers on them. Those were the days before Fremont Street was covered with a canopy, so there was plenty of room for crowds and bleachers. During Helldorado, I felt like a real cowboy.

Chapter 7: A Wonderful Life

Even though I retired from a fascinating photojournalism career, I never lost my passion for taking pictures. Life became an opportunity to pursue new adventures. I was free to travel and photograph whatever I desired. Whether the subject would be landscape, wildlife, or people, I was ready to seize the day.

I had two very nice trips in the summer of 2015. Needless to say, I took my camera with me both times. In June, we drove to Newport Beach and stayed three nights. While there, I wanted to take some pictures of the pier at dusk. It had been a long time since I saw the pier at night, so I was excited about the idea. We found a parking spot near the sand and walked toward the water's edge. I set up the tripod and snapped a few time exposure photos, meaning the shutter stayed open for about ten seconds. The photos were vibrant because of the blue color in the night sky and the movement of the waves.

A few days later, Debbie and I drove to San Diego. We went to the zoo and bought a backstage pass, which enabled us to feed a rhinoceros by hand. He was a very large animal and weighed about five thousand pounds. It was fun to actually touch him. In August, we traveled to northern California. We flew into San Francisco, rented a car, and drove to the Sonoma Valley wine country. Debbie had a friend who bought a Bed and Breakfast, so we stayed with her for three days. It was a very peaceful and beautiful area. After that, we drove back to San Francisco and stayed for a couple of days. We ate lunch at Scoma's restaurant on Fisherman's Wharf and had dinner with my trusty friend Mike Smithwick at the Palomino near the Ferry Building. One day, we drove to an old food staple where the locals eat called "Tommy's Joynt." It is the original Hof-Brau of San Francisco and has become one of the city's longest-living institutions. It was my kind of place. While in the city, I wanted to do some night photography. I positioned myself near the Ferry Building at 8:30 pm and took a few dusk shots of traffic moving under the Bay Bridge. I used the same exposure that I used in Newport Beach and got the same results. The movement of the cars on the street added to the success of the photos. I was very pleased with the outcome.

October of 2015 was a very happy month. The 1965 class from Bishop Gorman High School scheduled their 50th reunion, and Rossi asked for my help with the photography. Because I knew most of the people, I was happy to be involved. For me, it was a 3-day commitment. On the first day, basketball coach Bill Scoble held a luncheon for the team at the Las Vegas Country Club. It didn't take me long to recognize the old faces. Everybody looked pretty good. Rudy Basovsky, the coach of the baseball team, was also invited. I took a team photo, and the coach showed a video from one of their games. During lunch, there were speeches and stories that probably changed a little over time. After the event, each member of the team received a copy of the video and said their goodbyes. On the second day, I drove to Gorman for the Homecoming game. I arrived early and found a great parking space. That's unusual for a Gorman football game. The pre-game festivities took place on a field behind the football stadium. I found the right group and snapped some photos. Everyone seemed to enjoy themselves, and I blended right in. After all, it was also my alma mater. Just before the kickoff, we walked into the stadium and found some seats. The stadium looked like a very modern, high-tech place. It was much better than we had at the old campus. In fact, all we had was a small patch of weed-infested grass that the school used for physical education classes. Anyway, most of us left the game at half-time. The score was 55-0 in our favor. The final day of festivities took place at Rossi's home. He hosted a wonderful evening event. I got to the house early and took pictures of the set-up. There were tables in the backyard covered in orange and blue, a full bar, and a long buffet table. Inside were colorful decorations, coffee, and hors d'oeuvres. As guests arrived, the atmosphere became very festive. A lot more people attended the party than the two previous events. I took photos of Rossi's classmates during the cocktail hour. There was a lot of good conversation and fond memories.

After dinner, I took a group shot, and then Rossi cut into a cake. The evening was a huge success. People went away happy.

As November 2015 was winding down, the moon became full and bright in the winter sky. I decided to take advantage of the situation and capture some night photos of the desert. I talked Debbie into accompanying me on a trip to Red Rock Canyon. We drove into the darkness until we found a spot near Bonnie Springs Ranch. I parked the car and set my trusty Nikon D800E on a tripod. Although the temperature was a chilly 35 degrees, we dressed accordingly. I tested a few shots and then began taking the photos that I set out to create. The desert looked mysterious, and we could see a lot of stars. Each picture was better than the one before. I was enjoying the photo shoot until I heard some animal noises just beyond the sagebrush. As the sounds began to get closer, I decided it was time to leave. I quickly put my camera and tripod into the car and drove toward the city lights. Debbie and I talked all the way home. It was an enthralling adventure.

In March 2016, Debbie and I decided to revisit some of the nearby places that we had not seen in many years. We drove to the Valley of Fire for a day of hiking and photography. It was the right time of year for such an adventure because the intense summer heat was still a couple of months away. We discovered a few large lizards that were warming themselves in the afternoon sun. We also saw the beauty of the rock formations and desert plants in the state park. The Valley of Fire has a lot of sand. I was glad I took my hiking boots. Another day, we drove to the very small town of Nelson, located just outside of Boulder City. There are old cars, buildings, and other interesting items just waiting to be discovered. Local photographers use the location for backgrounds in photo albums, and video crews have used the props in movies. To me, it looked like a giant junkyard. I made the most of it and shot as many photos as I could in the time we had. Rusty cars in the desert make for great photos. Our last stop during Spring Break was Floyd Lamb Park at Tule Springs. It is a beautiful place just north of Las Vegas. The grounds are well-kept, and there's plenty of wildlife. Peacocks, geese, and ducks live among the historical buildings, and the lake is stocked with trout. The birds are very friendly. They eat crackers right out of your hands. I did take my camera and managed to get an exceptional picture of a Peacock showing his plumage.

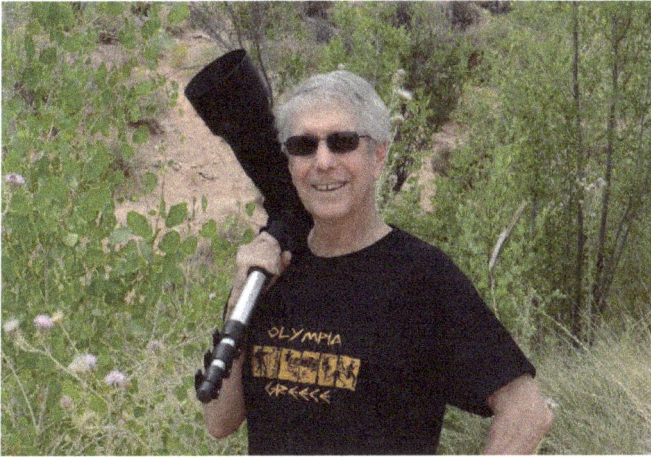

In the spring of 2016, I purchased a very large Nikon lens. I had used heavy lenses many times in the past, but I no longer had access to such exotic equipment. Therefore, I decided to buy a Nikkor 200-500mm zoom lens. Instead of sports, I planned to use it for wildlife photography. I began traveling to Red Rock Canyon a few times a week in search of anything that lived in the desert. Being a local, I knew which animals to expect. Wild burros, coyotes, jackrabbits, mountain lions, and assorted lizards were just waiting to be discovered. I found my best subjects near Bonnie Springs Ranch. A herd of wild burros lived in the area. I enjoyed taking pictures of the animals as they grazed and walked through the desert. After a few sessions, I began to know their habits. As long as I kept quiet and moved slowly, they ignored me. I photographed them from a distance of about 30 yards. If I tried to get closer, they simply moved a few yards further away. The only time they would be on high alert was when crowds of people stopped their cars and began making loud noises. That spooked the animals. It also disturbed me and what I was trying to accomplish. All in all, I captured many memorable pictures of the wild burros of Red Rock Canyon. A short distance down the road was the small village of Blue Diamond. Another herd of burros lived there, but the subject of my camera became the many jackrabbits that lived in a gully on the outskirts of town. The jackrabbits were larger than the local cottontails and had enormous ears. They were very fast and difficult to photograph. I was glad that I had a long lens. As July approached, the weather became very hot. I decided to suspend my quest for animal photos until the fall when the desert temperature would be more appealing.

In March 2016, I decided to find the person who used the name Coffee Jim Dandy on the radio during my younger years. After some internet research, I found a story about him in an old newspaper article. I discovered that his name was

Ken Wolt, but nothing else. Upon further research, I found his website. There was an email contact on the site, so I gave it a shot. To my delight, Ken answered me. He said that he was indeed Coffee Jim Dandy and that he had moved back to Las Vegas a few years ago. Since we were both golfers, we decided to meet for lunch at the Las Vegas Country Club. Lucky for me, he was a member. We had a wonderful visit. We each told stories of old Las Vegas and discovered that we had known mutual people. He also told me about his life. He owned radio stations, did some acting and voice-over work, and made more than 150 commercials. It sounded like Ken had a fulfilled life. He was also interested in my family. It had been a long time since someone wanted to know where my parents came from and how they ended up in Las Vegas. After lunch, Ken stayed at the golf course to hit some balls on the driving range, and I drove home with another fascinating Las Vegas story. After 50 years, I finally found Coffee Jim Dandy.

On May 22, 2016, I attended the graduation ceremony of Bishop Gorman High School. My class was invited to the event in celebration of our 50th year as Alumni. We were called the "Golden Grads" and were to walk into the Orleans Arena with the current senior class. Before the ceremony, we gathered in a room and received our gold-colored gowns. The current graduating boys wore blue, and the girls wore white. There were only 5 people from our class, but more than 300 from the current class. While waiting for the festivities to begin, we took photos with the bishop and talked with members of the school staff. When the time came, we marched into the auditorium behind the faculty but in front of the seniors. We took out designated seats and watched the ceremony. Before the diplomas were handed out, each of us was introduced. It was a nice touch. After the 2 hour event, we walked out and returned our gowns. All in all, it was a very nice day to be a graduate of Bishop Gorman High School.

On June 30, 2016, a woman named Claytee White from the Oral History Department at the University of Nevada Las Vegas arrived at my house. She wanted to interview me regarding the history of Las Vegas. She knew that I was a native of the area and would have pertinent information for her archives. I told stories about growing up in Las Vegas during the 1950s and 1960s. I also described the architecture of the hotels from that time period. We then talked about my working career from the 1970s to the day I retired in 2014. I showed her photos that I had taken while at the News Bureau and talked about some of the famous people I encountered while on my journey. All in all, the 3-hour interview went very well. I was happy to contribute to the History Department of UNLV.

Debbie and I traveled to Utah during the last few days of August 2016. We had never seen Zion National Park or

Bryce Canyon, so a trip was in order. We needed to get away from the hot summer air in Las Vegas, so we made reservations at the Zion Ponderosa Ranch outside the east entrance of the park. We left home early and arrived at Zion in about three hours. I used my Senior National Park Pass and saved the $30.00 entrance fee. We drove slowly through the park and stopped periodically to take photos. In the early afternoon, we checked into our cabin at the ranch. After getting the lay of the land, we had dinner and sat around a campfire, watching kids roast marshmallows. After that, we retired for the night. The next day was spent at the ranch. They had so many activities that we decided not to go anywhere else. We went on a one-hour trail ride, played horseshoes and miniature golf, and walked around the property taking pictures. That night, we went to a marshmallow roast, and I took some photos of the stars. The next day, we drove to Bryce Canyon. It was actually quite a spectacular sight. We hiked and took more scenic photos. Because of the elevation, it smelled like Lake Tahoe. Back at the ranch, we had a wonderful meal and enjoyed watching people zip-lining in the dark. The next morning, we checked out of the Ponderosa and drove through Zion to return home. It was raining, so the animals that inhabited the area were out looking for food. We were fortunate to see big horn sheep, herds of deer, wild turkeys, and a pronghorn antelope.

I had my 500mm lens, so I was in animal heaven. It was a short but enjoyable trip.

The weekend of October 15, 2016, was Homecoming for Bishop Gorman High School. Because it was the 50-year reunion of my class, I was very involved. A few months earlier, Yvette Robichaud and I became the committee that would organize the festivities. We planned a dinner at a restaurant named Grape Street Café in Downtown Summerlin. After much planning, shopping, and mailing, the weekend arrived. On Friday, some members of our class attended mass and a pep rally at the school. That night, we went to the football game and had a relaxing time. The next night was our dinner. More than 80 people attended. Some of us arrived early and decorated the restaurant with Gorman banners, footballs, and other accessories. We had a great time visiting, eating, and reminiscing about our days at Gorman. After dinner, we took a class photo outside the restaurant. It was a very special evening for all of us. It was nice to see each other after 50 years. The weekend was a success.

During the weekend of March 9, 2017, Debbie and I flew to Reno for an SAE event. It was the 100th anniversary of the Nevada Alpha Chapter at the University of Nevada. We arrived a few days early, rented a car, and drove to Lake Tahoe. We stayed at the Hyatt Hotel at Incline Village. It was a beautiful time of year, with lots of snow. While there, we had lunch in Truckee, drove around Donner Lake, and took a ride on the Dixie II to Emerald Bay. The weather was perfect, and there were no crowds. I took pictures of the lake, the river, and icicles on the rooftops. On Friday, we drove to Reno and checked into our hotel. We joined my fraternity brothers at Louie's Basque Restaurant that night for a cocktail reception. The next day, we met at the fraternity house and took a group photo, which I sent to our national headquarters for publication. Later that evening, we attended the formal banquet. It was a celebration of 100 years of friendship at the university. I had great conversations with many long-time friends. We sat at the same table with Sig Rogich and Bob Corkern and enjoyed a very nice event.

In 2017, I published another coffee table photo book. It was a collection of desert images that included ageless landscapes, diverse wildlife, and unique close-ups. I had been photographing the surrounding area for two years and put the best photos into a book entitled "Desert Colors." Most of the pictures were taken in southern Nevada, and they revealed the unique beauty of the desert. I photographed local areas, such as Red Rock Canyon and Spring Mountain Ranch. I also drove to Beatty, Goldfield, and Tonopah to find some interesting subjects. Debbie and I put on our hiking shoes and discovered a few very colorful objects in the land around Goldfield. We also spent the night at the Mizpah Hotel in Tonopah. While there, we walked around the old cemetery and toured mines that once produced the gold and silver that made Nevada famous. It was a great getaway and helped me put the finishing touches on the book. I enjoyed the project because it was a personal creation of beauty from my native land.

August 26, 2017, was a very sad day for our family. After 13 wonderful years, our beloved Kona passed away. She was a Chihuahua, a small dog with a big personality. She was a beautiful being, loving beyond love and trusting beyond trust. During my lifetime, I had several dogs, but none were as loyal, smart, and giving as Kona. She was a lap dog in every sense of the word. All she wanted out of life was to sit on my lap. In a family group, Chihuahuas choose one person to be their caregiver, and she chose me. I was honored to be her person. She had a devotion that I had never experienced. She also had a vocabulary beyond imagination. When I talked to her, she knew what I was saying. Kona was the best dog we could hope for, and she was my constant companion. I will never forget that little face looking up at me with unwavering love.

In the fall of 2017, Debbie and I decided to spend a few days in Newport Beach. It was a time to visit old friends. We stayed at the Hyatt for 3 nights. While there, we toured the harbor on a boat with Mike and Julie Cortney. We also enjoyed a nice dinner and took a ride in Mike's 1969 Corvette. Because we were in the area, we visited with our friend Mamie Van Doren. It had been years since we saw Mamie and Thomas, so it was quite a treat to sit with them and catch up on family stories. Mamie was in her mid 80's and looked incredible. After all, she made her living on her ageless beauty. Earlier in the day, we ran into Bill Medley in the parking lot of the Lido Isle shopping center. That was a nice surprise. We talked to Bill for a while, and then he got into his new white Jaguar and drove away. Debbie's brother also drove to Newport from Los Angeles and met us for lunch at our favorite Mexican restaurant. The trip was a great success.

During the winter of 2017, I continued my quest to find Nevada's famous Desert Bighorn Sheep. I knew where they lived but never had the privilege of seeing them. After a few trips to Boulder City, Debbie and I finally came across the herd. We stopped the car at Hemenway Park near Lake

Mead. There were about 25 magnificent Bighorn Sheep eating the grass. I gathered my camera and walked to a place near the sheep. They didn't seem to mind human interaction, as there were several other people enjoying the park. Although some were in the grassy area, many of the animals were sitting in the comfort of the nearby desert sand. I quickly began to photograph the sheep. As I took pictures, I noticed that they would only allow me to get within 30 yards of them. When I moved closer, they would quietly move away. They were animals that lived in the desert and would only tolerate human contact at a distance. I took hundreds of photos that day and was very happy with the results. As we were standing in the desert, the sheep decided they were finished eating and walked past us on their way back to the rugged mountains. It was a wonderful experience. Since then, we have seen them many times in the same area. I consider myself fortunate to have seen them up close and personal. Like the burros of Red Rock Canyon, the Desert Bighorn Sheep are peaceful, quiet, and cautious creatures. They are a sight to behold.

In January 2018, I turned 70 years old. My friend, Mike Cortney, also turned 70. We were born 3 days apart and have celebrated our birthdays together many times. Mike wanted to celebrate this birthday in Las Vegas, so he reserved several rooms at the Palazzo Hotel. He invited about 80 of his California friends to help celebrate the occasion. The group was in town for 4 days and enjoyed dinners and shows together. Debbie and I also attended the events. After the guests left town, Mike stayed an extra day. He came to our house, and we had another birthday dinner. It was a nice way to turn 70.

In the spring of 2018, Debbie and I took two road trips. We drove to Ely, Nevada, for a few days of relaxation. Since Las Vegas had very little cold weather during the winter, we wanted to see some snow. We were not disappointed. On the second day there, it snowed all night, and the countryside looked like a winter wonderland. I wanted to capture a photograph of the historic Ward Charcoal Ovens. They were built in 1876 to create charcoal for the railroad. They are currently part of the State Parks system. The 6 ovens are very picturesque, and I did get some fine shots. While there, we took a ride on the Northern Nevada Railroad train and spent some time at Cave Lake. It freezes in the winter, so it was quite a sight. Our next trip was to San Diego. We saw the San Diego Zoo, the Safari Park, the Liberty Station District, and the Point Loma Lighthouse. On this trip, I took all of my lenses. I captured great photos of the animals at the zoo, so I was very happy. As usual, the weather in San Diego was perfect.

In September 2018, we took another well-planned road trip to Ely. We had been there before, so we were prepared for the most rugged section of Nevada. It was a great opportunity for me to photograph wildlife. After driving to Ely, we traveled to Great Basin National Park. It is one of the most remote national parks in the country. We took a guided tour of the famous Lehman Caves and drove to the Wheeler Peak campgrounds. At the visitor's center, we had lunch consisting of the best barbecue chicken ever. The next day, I got out of bed at 5:30 am and drove to the White Pine Golf Course, directly behind our hotel. Once there, I captured some striking photographs of a family of Pronghorns. They are similar to antelope. It was not quite daylight, so the mood was perfect for wildlife photography. Later in the day, we drove to the Ward Charcoal Ovens and

Cave Lake. The fall colors were vivid, so my photos looked good. That night, we returned to Cave Lake to take photos of the night sky in all its glory. As we waited for the darkness, we saw 8 deer grazing directly in front of us. It was a very peaceful experience. During our trip, we stopped in the small town of Pioche to visit the grave of my dear friend Jim Kelly. The town had many Mule Deer roaming the streets. That road trip was fabulous.

There are some adventures that you simply can't resist. For me, riding a camel was one of them. I picked up a magazine that had a camel on the cover. Inside was an advertisement for a camel safari in the Nevada desert near the city of Mesquite. Debbie and I decided to take the 2-hour drive and partake in the adventure of a lifetime. We booked it online and drove to a remote ranch off the main highway. We were greeted by the friendly staff and signed the liability release. After a quick briefing, the camels were brought to us. They were magnificent critters, very tall and lanky. We climbed a few steps to a platform and mounted the camels. They were pretty well-behaved, as they were already television stars. A show called "The Bachelorette" featured them on one of their episodes. Suddenly, off we went into the surrounding desert. Each animal was guided by a single handler. Both of our handlers were from the Sahara Desert. We walked around the complex, looking at the other camels and vegetation that grew in the area. The time went quickly, and suddenly our ride was finished. We dismounted and received a tour of the property. It was a fun and unusual experience that we thoroughly enjoyed. On the drive home, I couldn't stop thinking about "Lawrence of Arabia."

In February 2019, there was a snowstorm in Red Rock Canyon. I had been waiting for the opportunity to photograph the desert covered with snow for a few years, and the time was finally right. Debbie and I drove to Bonnie

Springs Ranch early in the morning and found what we were looking for. I took a lot of photos of the snow-covered cactus. As a special added attraction, a few wild burros were wandering through the winter wonderland, and I was able to get some nice pictures of them. Snow in the desert is very special because it only lasts for a few hours. Sure enough, it disappeared quickly, and the desert was back to normal. Little did I realize that a much larger snowstorm would blanket the Las Vegas valley a few days later. The snow began to fall Thursday afternoon and intensified as the night temperatures dropped. The next day, we got up early and drove to our favorite spot near Bonnie Springs. On this day, the desert was a complete whiteout. Each cactus was covered in heavy snow, and I captured the desert scenery with many unique photos. It was a great week for Las Vegas residents, many of whom played in the fresh snow.

While awaiting springtime, Mike and Julie came to town. We planned a dinner at Bob Taylor's Ranch House. It was built in 1955 and now has the distinction of being the oldest restaurant in the city. We all ordered steaks and had a fabulous time. A few days later, we took a day trip to Death Valley. We wanted to see if there were any wildflowers blooming. The forecast predicted rain, and it was already cloudy when we arrived. Our first stop was Zabriskie Point, a well-known site for photography. As we hiked and took photos, it began to rain. The surrounding countryside transformed into an artistic wonderland as the wet rocks burst with colors. I managed to get some outstanding pictures, so I was very happy. Suddenly, the drizzle of rain turned into a steady downpour. We wanted to drive on the road to the wildflowers, but it was closed due to flooding. It was lunchtime, so we went to the restaurant at Furness Creek Ranch. We had a leisurely meal, hoping the rain would let up. It only intensified. There were rumors of more road closures, so we got into the car and headed back to Las Vegas. It only rains a few days a year in Death Valley, and we just happened to be there on one of them. All in all, it was a nice day trip. Death Valley is always a unique experience.

We discovered a great restaurant in the village of Blue Diamond named Cottonwood Station. It opened in April of 2018 and was about to celebrate its first anniversary. The eatery served delicious food and became our favorite place for breakfast and lunch. It was a short drive from our house, just past the Red Rock loop. Each time we drove there, it seemed like a mini vacation. Nevada Magazine was preparing a story on the restaurant, so I offered to take photos to accompany the article. I shot interiors, exteriors, and food shots. The owners, Jody and Steve, were very accommodating and happily assisted. Soon after the photo shoot, I sent a nice selection to the magazine. They selected the food and interior shots. A few weeks later, the May/June issue of Nevada Magazine hit the newsstands. The layout was well done.

During my photo trips to Red Rock Canyon, I saw a lot of wildlife. The desert lizards were fast and playful, and the birds of prey were amazing. They flew high and were difficult to photograph. Once, I managed to capture a hawk on the ground with my camera. It was a colorful and dramatic shot. After that, I searched the internet for a place where I could actually interact with birds of prey. I found a raptor experience in Ramona, California, just north of San Diego. Debbie and I decided to sign up for their raptor program. We drove to Ramona and found the location. We were greeted by the proprietor named Terry. She introduced us to a magnificent hawk, and then we took turns enticing the bird to our gloved arm with bite-size treats. He was a 2-year-old male who would land gently on the glove, eat the treat and pose for a photo. The raptor would then fly up into a tree and wait for the next treat. We repeated this many times, took a lot of photos, and had great fun. After that, Debbie and I sat in the shade of a large tree and awaited the next bird. Terry brought out a barn owl. It had very interesting brown feathers and a white face. The owl wasn't allowed to fly like the hawk; it would not have come back. We took turns holding the barn owl, took more photos, and listened to Terry talk about her birds. She explained the difference between owls and hawks and their specific diets.

Next, Terry brought out a very large owl with golden eyes. I think it was a Great Horned Owl. We listened to stories about this amazing bird but were not allowed to hold it. Soon, our experience with the raptors was over. We had a great time with the birds of prey and talked about our experience for the rest of the trip.

The more I photographed desert creatures, the more I appreciated them. Chipmunks, roadrunners, and jackrabbits were always on my radar because they were plentiful and easy to spot. Chipmunks are inquisitive and playful. They gather around picnic tables and look for morsels they can stuff into their cheeks. Then, the little rodents carry their treasure to a burrow to be stored for later use. Roadrunners are birds that spend most of their time on the ground. They're very quiet and can cover a lot of ground while on the run. Of the many roadrunner photos I've taken, one, in particular, was the most dramatic. A roadrunner jumped into a shrub.

He perched there for a few seconds, and I got the photo. It was the only time I saw a roadrunner off the ground. Jackrabbits, which are actually hares, are much larger than cottontails. They are solitary creatures and keep their distance. Because I had a telephoto lens, I was able to get pictures of them. Their trademark ears are a sight to behold. I believe the writer Mark Twain brought their name to fame by using it in his western stories. Trying to keep up with the jackrabbits was always a good workout.

One autumn day, while driving through Red Rock Canyon, I turned into Bonnie Springs Ranch to photograph the colors on the desert floor. As I came to a stop, I noticed a single burro standing on the side of the road. He approached my car and stuck his head through the passenger side window. My camera was not within reach, so I began to gently scratch his face. After a while, I got out of the car and walked toward the burro. He seemed to enjoy my company, so I began scratching his back. I could tell that he was an older gent because of his appearance and body language. He had scars on his neck and was very dusty. It seemed we were both veterans of life, meandering through the late afternoon. His battle scars were from barbed wire fences and fights with other wild burros. Mine were from sports injuries and prolonged sun exposure. After a while, he slowly walked away, and our encounter was over. In a strange way, I felt we had bonded. We were both born and raised in the area and were nearing the end of our journey. As he disappeared into the desert landscape, I brushed the dust from my clothes and drove away, wondering if our paths would cross again. I hoped so.

In October 2019, Debbie and I decided to take a brief trip out of town before the winter holidays. We flew into Reno to relax in northern Nevada. During our stay, we visited Genoa, Lake Tahoe, and Virginia City. A cold spell set in during our trip, but it didn't stop us. We were prepared for the weather. On the first day, we drove to Genoa, the oldest town in Nevada. It is a small, rural town that boasts the oldest saloon in the state. We took photos of the bar and ate lunch in a local deli. The next day, we traveled to Lake Tahoe. After a wonderful breakfast in the town of Truckee, we drove along the river toward our destination. At Lake Tahoe, we stopped at Emerald Bay and Sand Harbor. They are the most scenic spots on an alpine lake. Because it was the off-season, there were very few people in the area. On the last day of our trip, we spent in Virginia City with my college friends, Mike Smithwick and Monae DeVille. While there, Mike and Monae bought western hats, and we all purchased some fudge from a candy store. We had a great time visiting for hours in the Bucket of Blood Saloon. It was a surprisingly bright and friendly place. After the day in Virginia City, we had dinner in the steakhouse of our hotel. The next day, Debbie and I flew home, filled with wonderful photos and memories.

Northern Mockingbirds are lively little guys that constantly chatter, sometimes all night long. The slender-bodied gray birds pour all their energy into their personalities, as they can mimic many different sounds. I always enjoyed having them in my neighborhood, but the spring of 2020 was a special treat. A pair of mockingbirds built a nest near our house. Soon, the eggs hatched, and the parents became very busy feeding the new arrivals. I knew their diet consisted of fruit and bugs, so I began placing grapes on the wall in the backyard. I would pinch the grapes into small pieces and put a few on top of the fence. The birds would eat a couple of bites and then take the grapes to the babies in the nest. I started feeding them every day, and it became a ritual. Suddenly, I found them sitting on the wall every morning, awaiting their breakfast. As time went on, they allowed me to get very close to them when I served the grapes. In fact, I developed a certain whistle that they recognized. Each time I called, the birds would glide down from the trees and land on the wall. For wild birds, it was fascinating. Most days, I would sit in my yard and photograph the birds for hours. Soon, the babies began to realize the feeding ritual and started eating the grapes on their own. All in all, it was a wonderful experience. They never did let me touch them, but I enjoyed every minute of it. That spring, I took some great photos and had a lot of fun with the Northern Mockingbirds of Southern Nevada.

Wednesday, May 5, was a clear evening at Cave Lake in the spring of 2021. I was there to photograph the night sky in this remote section of Nevada. At about 8:00 pm, I set my camera on a tripod and waited for it to get dark. After a few minutes, the stars were shining, and I began to take photos. Everyone in our group was enjoying peace and tranquility when a strange sight appeared. Ten objects were moving across the sky in a straight line. We watched in amazement as they slowly moved overhead. Then, twenty more began to glide into view. Being from Las Vegas, I thought I had seen it all, but this was something very different. It was eerie, to say the least. It took about five minutes for the ghostly figures to complete their overhead journey. Then, they were gone. We were close to Area 51, so Dave, Carolyn, Debbie, and I thought about UFOs invading our galaxy. As Earthlings, we did not want to be captured and taken into the unknown, so we hurriedly packed our belongings and drove back to the hotel in Ely. On the way, we made a pact, never to mention what we had just seen. I, for one, believe anything is possible, so I kept quiet and repented for my past sins. Later that night, Dave researched strange sightings in the night sky. He discovered that a satellite train had caused some excitement across the entire country. They were satellites launched by Elon Musk's SpaceX as part of its Starlink internet service, and the mystery at Cave Lake was solved.

During the summer of 2021, the Desert Bighorn Sheep made their daily appearance at Hemenway Park near Boulder City. The sheep did not like sudden noise or movements, so most people were respectful and watched them quietly. I couldn't pass up the opportunity to photograph these interesting animals. The herd numbered about thirty-five. One cool and overcast day, I witnessed a sheep running into the park from the desert, leaping for joy. Fortunately, I had my camera pointed in the right direction and captured a once-in-a-lifetime photo. I had never seen a sheep jump that high. The females weigh about 125 pounds, and the rams weigh 200 pounds, so I always give them plenty of space. They are wild animals, and you can't predict their behavior. During another trip to the park, I photographed a baby standing next to his parents. That image became my favorite photo of the summer. It's always thrilling to spend time with Nevada's Bighorns, especially with a camera in your hand.

I had taken so many photos of the Desert Bighorn Sheep that Debbie and I began making greeting cards out of them. One day, while having coffee in Boulder City, I showed them to the owner of The Boulder City Company Store. She liked the idea and agreed to sell them in her business. They sold so well that she also requested greeting cards from nearby Hoover Dam. Needless to say, I photographed the dam from every angle and turned the photos into cards. The Bighorn Sheep and the Hoover Dam cards are now selling in Boulder City. There is also a bookstore and coffee shop a few blocks from The Company Store called the Dam Roast House. The owner agreed to sell my latest book of poetry entitled "There's Nobody In The Director's Chair." He bought a few copies and placed them on the shelf with other local authors. For some reason, I've had good luck showing my creations in Boulder City. It has a small-town vibe, where people move slowly and appreciate the arts. At my age, I enjoy staying active. Showing my photography and writing gives me a nice outlet.

The year 2022 started off very well. Debbie and I traveled to Jackson Hole, Wyoming, with our next-door neighbors, Terry and Jeanette. Because the winter was so mild here, we wanted to experience the snow. We flew on Delta Airlines and stayed at a nice Bed & Breakfast called Inn on the Creek. While in Wyoming, we managed to see an abundance of wildlife. We rode on a horse-drawn wagon through the nearby Elk refuge, and I was able to get some photographs. We also hired a local driver who took us to a secret pond where a group of Trumpeter Swans lived. Jackson Hole is known for its scenery and wildlife, and we saw plenty of both. I was especially fascinated with all of the moose standing near the roads. They were easy to photograph. We ate good food, bought plenty of souvenirs, and walked in the snow. To top it off, the Bed & Breakfast was owned by the Mayor. She cooked breakfast for us each day.

Two months later, we drove to Ely to ride the Nevada Northern Railway trains. We stayed at The Prospector Hotel and had tickets for the Star Train Experience. At sunset, a diesel train took us a few miles out of town to view the dark sky in northeastern Nevada. The Park Rangers set up telescopes for the passengers, and everyone enjoyed the view. I took my tripod and captured some pretty good photos. The next day, we rode the train again. This time, it was a steam locomotive built in 1917. The passengers were treated to a Wild West Show and robbed of their possessions by local bandits. On this trip to Ely, Debbie and I finally saw "Dirt the Cat." He is the mascot of the railroad and is sometimes difficult to find. We found him sitting near his bed in the Engine House. He came over to us and posed for a few photos. It was a good day. While on the road, we planted wildflowers at the gravesite of my friend Jim Kelly in Pioche. We also stopped near Area 51 and took some photos of an alien from outer space. It was just a tall statue, but it made for some fun photographs. Being a desert dweller myself, I appreciated the humor that my newfound friend brought to the landscape.

After the summer heat, we decided it was time for another Nevada road trip. I was still searching for the Milky Way, so we drove to Tonopah for a dark sky. It was September, and the chance of seeing the Milky Way was good. On the way, we stopped in Goldfield, the site of a major gold discovery in 1904. By 1908 Goldfield had become Nevada's largest city, with a population of 20,000. Today fewer than 300 people live in the area. It's considered a living ghost town. Debbie and I spent a few hours in Goldfield, talking to the locals and visiting the historic sites.

A point of interest was the cemetery. It was very large, and the headstones were interesting. Like many people in those days, gunshots were the cause of their departure from life. Of the hundreds of headstones in the cemetery, one is the most photographed. It seems that an unknown man died from eating library paste in 1908. We looked for the grave for quite a while but couldn't find it. I was beginning to think it was just an old wives' tale. After all, who would eat library paste? We then continued on the road to Tonopah. Once we arrived, we checked into the historical and sometimes haunted Mizpah Hotel. Built-in 1907, the Mizpah was one of the first luxury hotels in Nevada. Today, it still remains the centerpiece of the city. The two days we spent in Tonopah were actually very nice. We visited historical museums, met new friends, enjoyed the local restaurants and took lots of photos. Tonopah was the site of one of the richest booms in the west. In 1900, a man named Jim Butler discovered gold and silver in the area. Soon after that, prospectors flocked to Tonopah to work in the mines. Currently, only turquoise is mined on a small scale. While visiting the Central Nevada Museum, we met the man in charge of the headstones in the Goldfield cemetery. As luck would have it, he told us the exact location of the elusive library paste headstone. With that knowledge, we were determined to find it on the way home. That afternoon, people were gathering in the fabulous lobby and bar area of the Mizpah Hotel. The locals were having cocktails after work, but the inquisitive tourists were preparing for the star party that would take place after dark. Tonopah has a designated stargazing park just off the main street. It is a large cement pad designed to accommodate telescopes and photo tripods. For me, the time had finally arrived. The Milky Way would be visible in the night sky. At dusk, we drove to the park. I set up my tripod and camera while Debbie visited with the other adventurers. In a few minutes, the Milky Way appeared, and I captured it. After searching for years, my quest was complete. The photos looked good, and I was happy. The next day, we checked out of the Mizpah and headed for home. Knowing that our road trip was not quite finished, we stopped at the Goldfield cemetery. After a short walk from the car, we spotted the famous headstone. The engraving on the old stone said, "Unknown man died eating library paste July 14, 1908." I took photos of the coins and rocks people had left in tribute to the unknown man. It was not a myth or ghoulish tale; it was real. We were elated with our discovery, and our mission was accomplished. That afternoon, we arrived home with stories of our own. Nevada road trips are always filled with some kind of adventure.

In early autumn, Mamie Van Doren called to inform me that the book she had been working on was finally available on Amazon. The book entitled "China & Me" is the story of her relationship with a pet Cockatoo and other animals she's had throughout her life. I had a sneak peek months ago and was as excited as Mamie about the finished product. A few days later, my autographed copy arrived in the mail. I thoroughly enjoyed reading it and was honored to be mentioned in the dedication. It was a heartfelt project for Mamie. She is a very special person. I am happy for her.

For the last few years, I've been attending a quarterly breakfast at the Omelet House on Charleston Boulevard. The gathering is called "The Legends Breakfast," and it is hosted by Kevin Mills, owner of the restaurant. Long-time Las Vegas residents come together for camaraderie and stories. We not only celebrate the past but embrace the prosperity of our modern spirited city. Each of us has unique stories, and we love sharing them. The tales probably get embellished as time goes by, but that's the charm of it all. Everyone attending is a legend in their own way. Politicians, entertainers, business owners, and plain folks enjoy the food and relaxation. Former Senator Richard Bryan, Former Sheriff Ralph Lamb, Legendary basketball coach Jerry Tarkanian, and many others have taken their seats at the table over the years. Former Mayor Oscar and current Mayor Carolyn Goodman are the first to speak, followed by the rest of us. With such a diverse group, breakfast is always entertaining. For me, it is an honor to be invited to such a joyous event.

I'm the kind of person who enjoys keeping in touch. There is a special group of high school friends whom I have lunch or dinner with once in a while. On the last day of September, my wonderful classmates gathered at a restaurant called Brio. Patty Hirsch Schumacher, Madelyn Naples Montgomery, Angie Blasco Becker, and Michele Borsack Morrison were in attendance. We enjoyed good food and a very nice conversation. It was one of those rare and great moments in time that we all appreciated. A few weeks later, we gathered for dinner at The Italian American Club. This time Madelyn, Angie, Mike Cortney, and Coach Bill Scoble were there, along with a few spouses. The dinner house is an iconic Las Vegas staple. For Debbie and me, it had been a long time since we enjoyed a meal there. That night was one of the best of the year, very special indeed.

Well, here's where the stories end. During my lifetime, I took some photos, published a few books, and had many interesting jobs. I was lucky enough to watch a full moon rise over the Golden Gate Bridge, shop the famous Miracle Mile in Chicago, and stroll the sidewalks of New York. I swam with stingrays in the Cayman Islands, glided through the kelp forests of Catalina Island, and drifted through the waters of Hawaii. I rode in hot air balloons, helicopters, and blimps. I attended a World Series baseball game and two All-Star games. I've also watched a small desert town called Las Vegas transform itself into a truly international destination. I've been extremely fortunate, and for that, I am grateful. While writing this manuscript, I tried to recall the people and events that shaped my life. Although I missed a few, at least you have a glimpse into what it was like growing up in a fascinating place known as "Glitter Gulch."

www.ingramcontent.com/pod-product-compliance
Lightning Source LLC
Chambersburg PA
CBHW041820090426
42811CB00009B/1050